Hood Canal Press
Redmond, WA

Enterprise Data Synchronization with Microsoft SQL Server 2008 and SQL Server Compact 3.5

Mobile Merge Replication

Rob Tiffany
Mobility Architect
Microsoft

> Dedication

I wrote this book on airplanes and in hotels as I travelled the globe helping some of the world's greatest companies mobilize their workforces with SQL Server, Merge Replication, .NET and SQL Server Compact.

I want to thank my wife and family for being so supportive of these endeavors.

Enterprise Data Synchronization with Microsoft SQL Server 2008 and SQL Server
Compact 3.5 Mobile Merge Replication
Copyright © 2009 by Hood Canal Press

ISBN-13: 978-0-9798912-1-2
ISBN-10: 0-9798912-1-3

Library of Congress Control Number: 2007940751
Library of Congress Cataloging-in-Publication Data
Tiffany, Rob
  Enterprise Data Synchronization with Microsoft SQL Server 2008 and SQL Server
  Compact 3.5 Mobile Merge Replication / Rob Tiffany
  ISBN: 0-9798912-1-3

  1.   Microsoft SQL Server 2. Database Management 3. Microsoft .NET Framework 4.
        Computers

Created, encoded, printed and bound in the United States of America

Hood Canal Press books are available through booksellers and distributors worldwide. For further information contact Hood Canal Press at http://www.hoodcanalpress.com.

Windows Mobile, SQL Server 2008, the .NET Compact Framework and SQL Server Compact 3.5 are either registered trademarks or trademarks of Microsoft Corporation in the United States and/or other countries. Other product and company names mentioned herein may be the trademarks of their respective owners.

The authors and publisher have taken care in the preparation of this book but make no expressed or implied warranty of any kind and assume no responsibility for errors or omissions. No liability is assumed for incidental or consequential damages in connection with or arising out of the use of the information or programs contained herein. The example companies, organizations, products, domain names, e-mail addresses, logos, people, places, and events depicted herein are fictitious. No association with any real company, organization, product, domain name, e-mail address, logo, person, place, or event is intended or should be inferred.

> Table of Contents

> About the Author

Rob Tiffany is an Architect at Microsoft focused on delivering the best possible Windows Mobile solutions for his customers. His expertise lies in combining wireless data technologies, Windows phones, and optimized server infrastructures together to form compelling solutions. Prior to his current role, Rob was a Senior Technical Product Manager for Windows Mobile in Microsoft's Mobile and Embedded Devices division where he grew the mobile developer ecosystem. He was also responsible for planning and running one of Microsoft's largest global developer conferences. Prior to joining Microsoft, Rob founded one of the industry's first mobile device management companies.

A writer, speaker, entrepreneur and 15-year veteran of the software industry, Rob has been involved in some of the world's largest Mobile/Wireless Line of Business application efforts undertaken to date. He's the creator of Microsoft's Mobile Line of Business Solution Accelerator, the author of "SQL Server CE Database Development with the .NET Compact Framework" plus dozens of articles found in leading software development publications. He's presented sessions on mobile development, infrastructure, and architecture at events all over the world including Tech Ed, Dev Connections, TechReady, VS Live, and MEDC. He got his start in programming by creating completely useless BASIC applications on the Timex Sinclair 1000 in the early 1980's. Luckily, he moved on to bigger and better things like 32-bit REXX on OS/2. Rob blogs at http://blogs.msdn.com/robtiffany.

> Contributors

Darren Shaffer

Darren Shaffer is the Chief Software
Architect at Handheld Logic and a
Microsoft Device Development MVP.
Darren is responsible for the design and development of over 50
.NET Compact Framework and Smart Client solutions for Fortune
1000 companies in the past five years. Darren is a frequent
speaker at Global Microsoft Events such as MEDC and Tech Ed as
well as a contributor to MSDN, emphasizing the importance of the
.NET Compact Framework, SQL CE/SQL Mobile, and teaching
mobile development best practices. Darren moderates the MSDN
SQL Compact Edition forum, and is a published author on a
number of .NET mobile development topics. A West Point
graduate and retired Army Telecommunications Officer, Darren
now lives in Colorado with his wife and daughter.

Michael Jimenez

Michael Jimenez has been in IT infrastructure
support, professional training, and consulting
services, for over fifteen years. Michael has had
the opportunity to evangelize, architect, plan, &
deploy, Microsoft mobility solutions for many large enterprise
customers around the globe. Currently, Michael is a Mobility
Solutions Architect within Microsoft Consulting Services and has
presented sessions at MEC, Techready, MEDC, and MMS. Michael
blogs at http://blogs.technet.net.com/mjimenez.

> Acknowledgements

The biggest outside help I received in creating this newest book on Merge Replication came from **Chris Fussell** and **Brian Jackson** who helped me push the envelope when it comes to SQL Server performance analysis. You guys rock! I also want to thank **Jean-Yves Devant** and **Vijay Tandra Sistla** who helped deepen my understanding of what's going on under the hood.

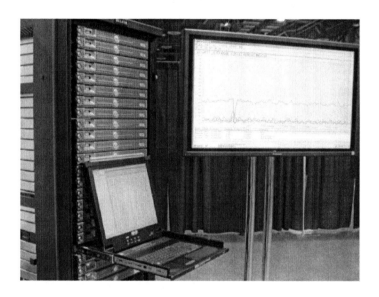

A big thanks also goes out to **Darren Flatt, Ginny Caughey, Darren Shaffer, Loke Uei Tan, Dave Bottomley, Michael Jimenez, Rabi Satter, Tim McAffee** and **Steve Hegenderfer** for staffing my Merge Replication booth at MEDC, Tech Ed, Dev Connections and TechReady events throughout the last few years. You all did a great job teaching the hundreds of curious attendees how to build out a scalable mobile line of business infrastructure. Also, thank you to John Dietz for supporting the notion that "Seeing is Believing," thus allowing me to assemble this travelling road show of enterprise Mobility.

> Foreword

In the past 14 years of working with data synchronization, I have seen a lot of interesting implementations. Before joining Microsoft's synchronization group, I worked with Sybase iAnywhere and remember working with a trucking company that had to "super" ruggedize their mobile devices to counteract drivers who liked to stress test the devices by first driving over them with their 18 wheelers. Then there was the time I helped set up wireless LANs in a golf course (back in the early days of wireless) to allow golfers to track the scores of their competitors on mobile devices only to see a golfer make a beautiful drive right into one of our main wireless hubs. Luckily it handled it quite well (although I can't say it faired quite as well when the homes surrounding the course started turning on the microwaves early in the morning).

Since this time, mobile devices have come a long way. They no longer are just being used by business users for email and contact management. Devices can now handle gigabytes of data and companies are building extremely sophisticated applications such as remote collaboration applications and mobile business intelligence dashboards for workers to locally analyze and report on data using technologies like Merge Replication and Microsoft Sync Framework. As we move forward, we are seeing more and more new applications and an increasing trend in consumer based data synchronization applications.

Through all of this, there are two key things that I have learned. The first is that most people underestimate the value of being able to get data regardless of data connectivity and second, like I found with the golf scoring application, data synchronization is a lot more difficult to implement than you would think.

Merge Replication has long provided the ability for companies to build these types of offline applications. It provides all of the tools a company needs to build an effective data synchronization solution. Unfortunately, as mentioned earlier, synchronization is much more difficult than many people might think. Luckily there are people like Rob Tiffany there to help us understand the best practices that help to build an effective and scalable system.

This book is a culmination of the many years Rob has invested traveling the world and working with customers building scalable data synchronization solutions. I believe this is a great book for anyone looking to understand the techniques and best practices behind building a synchronization solution using Merge Replication.

Liam Cavanagh
Senior Lead Program Manager
Microsoft Sync Framework and Cloud Data Services

Chapter 1 > Let's Dive In

Introduction to Mobile Merge Replication

The global trend of organizations mobilizing their respective workforces has become a tidal wave, with laptops outselling desktops and mobile phones outselling all computer platforms combined. With workers un-tethered from their desks and offices, the "virtual office" of the late 1990s is now the mainstream way of doing business for most companies. Organizations have boosted their agility by pushing out critical business functions to the point of activity where employees are empowered to make timely decisions and perform tasks that best serve both the interests of their customers, as well as their own company. This repudiation of the traditional "connected" software application model has increased customer satisfaction, boosted worker efficiency, reduced "missed opportunities" and resulted in cost savings, as un-wired employees get their jobs done wherever they happen to be.

With the Ethernet cable unplugged and replaced by local and wide area wireless networks, organizations now find themselves needing to take the applications they use to run their business "offline." No software application in the world better personifies the "occasionally-connected" model needed to succeed in today's mobile environment than Microsoft Outlook. Its ability to synchronize email, contacts and calendars keeps laptop, tablet and mobile phone users productive even when wireless connectivity doesn't exist. This works because Microsoft Outlook always works with local data, doesn't assume connectivity, and synchronizes with Microsoft Exchange Server, when the network is available.

The mobile line of business equivalent to Microsoft Outlook and Exchange Server would be a .NET application running on a laptop, tablet or Windows phone. It always works with local data stored in SQL Server Compact, it doesn't assume connectivity, and it synchronizes with Microsoft SQL Server when the network is available. Merge Replication is a data synchronization technology that's built into SQL Server and SQL Server Compact, facilitating the "occasionally-connected" line of business application needed to empower your mobile workforce. The substantial time and expense of staffing a large development team to construct custom mobile middleware is replaced by "wizard-driven" configuration of data synchronization settings, providing faster time to market. Finally, unlike a custom-created solution, Merge Replication is a Microsoft-supported technology.

Two of the most important elements in creating an offline, mobile line of business application are the presence of a mobile data store, coupled with an enterprise database with which it can synchronize. Going all the way back to SQL Server 6.0 for Windows NT in 1995, Microsoft's flagship enterprise database has come equipped with a mature, sophisticated data-synchronization technology called Merge Replication. Using a hub-and-spoke architecture, this technology is used to replicate data from a Publication database to Subscriber databases, which make changes and then merge back their inserts, updates and deletes into their Publication database. Changes can also be made to the Publication database directly whether or not the Subscriber databases are connected. SQL Server captures all incremental data changes and reconciles conflicts according to rules you configure, or via a custom resolver you create. This technology is a perfect fit to push out corporate data to branch offices where autonomous changes on both sides can be made, reconciled and then merged back together over wide-area private circuits or VPN tunnels.

With the introduction of SQL Server CE 1.0 back in 2001, Merge Replication evolved from being a server-to-server technology to one which embraced Pocket PC devices, as well. Utilizing Internet standards, the SQL Server team created a firewall-friendly synchronization transport protocol utilizing HTTP, SSL and Internet Information Services (IIS) to reach not only Pocket PC devices on the wireless LAN, but also those intermittently-online and -offline devices found roaming wireless WANs. With SQL Server CE supporting Merge Replication right out of the box, the Pocket PC instantly became the mobile line of business platform of choice, when combined with development tools such as Embedded Visual Basic, Embedded C++ and the .NET Compact Framework. Since 2001, SQL Server has revved from 2000 to 2005 to 2008 and SQL Server CE has matured to SQL Server Compact Edition (SSCE) 3.5 SP1. With each version update, the data synchronization technology has become faster, more scalable, more efficient over slow networks and better able to recover from loss of connectivity. Today, Merge Replication stands out as the most advanced data synchronization technology in a crowded field of competitors. No other sync solution offers the breadth and depth of functionality, manageability and performance.

Are there alternatives to this kind of replication to keep data synchronized with SSCE? Sure, but there's no silver bullet:

- The use of the **ADO.NET SQL Server driver** in the .NET Compact Framework allows Windows Mobile devices to talk directly to the database. This solution is best suited to corporate WLAN environments that can guarantee complete Wi-Fi coverage campus-wide, because there's no automatic recovery from network dropouts. It's not a WWAN solution since the device must talk directly to SQL Server via port 1433. Also, it can't support the resolution of conflicts the way Merge Replication can.

- **Remote Data Access (RDA)** is the younger sibling of Merge Replication. It utilizes a brute-force approach to not only get data from SQL Server to SSCE on the device, but also to post changes back to the server. It uses a "last-in, overwrite all others" form of optimistic concurrency. In other words, you lose the smart-conflict resolution and change tracking you get with Merge Replication. You have to write code to pull down each table, but you don't get referential integrity or the ability to use Identity columns for primary keys. Additionally, RDA doesn't support the downloading of database change deltas; therefore, you must drop and re-download each table to refresh your local database. With the advent of Sync Services for ADO.NET, RDA is now considered a deprecated technology.

- **Web Services** can be used with custom XML schemas or serialized DataSets and would give you an SOA solution to this problem. This would give you complete control over your server API and is one way to communicate with other enterprise databases. The problem is that you'll have to write thousands of lines of middleware code to reproduce the built-in functionality of Merge Replication. Additionally, web services don't do a good job of moving large amounts of data over the air and don't offer any recovery from network dropouts.

- **Sync Services for ADO.NET** is Microsoft's latest sync technology that utilizes the DataSet as its wire protocol. This developer-focused component of the Microsoft Sync

Framework you build in Visual Studio allows SSCE to synchronize with any database that supports ADO.NET. This means you can finally add Oracle and DB2 to the family of databases with which SQL Server Compact can sync. Obviously it can sync with SQL Server 2005, but it really shines when it taps into SQL Server 2008's efficient, new change-tracking engine that doesn't require the creation of triggers to keep tables in sync.

- **Live Mesh** is a higher-level synchronization technology from Microsoft that utilizes the FeedSync protocol created by Ray Ozzie and used with Windows Azure in the cloud. With Live Mesh, you can have folders on Windows, the Mac, Windows Mobile and the Web, all synchronize their contents with each other. For instance, whenever I take a picture with my Windows phone, Live Mesh could automatically send that picture back to the photo gallery residing on my Windows 7 PC at home.

Scenarios

While it is important to know that Merge Replication can synchronize your enterprise data between SQL Server in the data center and SSCE on laptops, tablets and Windows Mobile, it might be helpful to illustrate scenarios where this kind of technology can add value to your organization:

- **Sales Force Automation**
  A salesperson has leads that are filtered for her particular region and replicated to her device so she knows whom to contact in her area. Upon converting a lead to a sale, the Salesperson can fill out required data for a new client on

her Windows phone and then immediately replicate that data back to her organization's headquarters.

- **Healthcare**
Upon having a new patient assigned to him at a hospital, the doctor can securely replicate the patient's records down to his Tablet PC for review. At the point of diagnosis, the doctor can enter the symptoms, diagnosis, course of treatment and any prescriptions into his Tablet PC for immediate synchronization back to the primary patient records database. At this point, the pharmacist can replicate down the new prescription for the patient to her Windows Vista desktop and have it filled.

- **Supply Chain Management**
Upon receiving a phone call to place a new order for hardware, the customer service representative enters the order into her Windows 7 laptop and then synchronizes the information with the central database. A warehouse "picker" synchronizes his Windows Mobile barcode scanner and finds out that he needs to pick some hardware products from the various bins located in the warehouse. Upon completion, he synchronizes with the central database, thus alerting the forklift driver that there are staged items waiting to be loaded into a delivery truck. The forklift driver loads the ordered hardware onto the truck, updates his vehicle-mounted Windows CE device and replicates. Early the next morning, the route delivery driver arrives at the distribution center and syncs his ruggedized Windows Mobile device. His device tells him what items have been loaded on his truck and to which customers he will deliver. After receiving a proof of

delivery signature on his device, he will replicate the competed-order information back to the central database so that accounts receivable can invoice the customer.

- **Retail**
A sales associate at a clothing store notices that the line at the checkout counter has grown extremely long and customers are becoming impatient. She gets her Windows Mobile device with attached, magnetic-stripe reader and transforms herself into a portable point-of-sale checkout location to relieve the backed-up lines. As she checks out customers, her device replicates the changes in clothing inventory to the inventory management database, while simultaneously synchronizing the sales receipts with her company's accounting database. Keep in mind, that when you go to the Apple Store to buy an iPhone, this is exactly how they will check you out. Yes, they have to use Windows Mobile to take care of business.

- **Maintenance**
It's a particular plant worker's job to walk around an oil refinery, reading gauges and observing the health of equipment. He goes from logging that information on his clipboard, to entering the data into his Tablet PC. Via Merge Replication, he can instantly notify his superiors or the spare parts department if he finds faulty equipment or gauges which aren't properly calibrated.

- **Emergency Management**
First responders arriving on the scene of a disaster can use their Windows Mobile devices to take pictures, enter information about what they find, and then replicate that data back to their agency's headquarters. Furthermore, to

prevent the creation of data "silos," SQL Server on the back-end can replicate peer-to-peer with other agency databases to ensure that pertinent information is shared with everyone who needs it. That same data can be replicated back out to on-the-scene first responders from other government agencies to provide insight into what their inter-agency counterparts have discovered.

- **Restaurants**
  Waiters and waitresses normally take your dinner order by writing it down on paper or memorizing it. Once they walk back to the kitchen, they hang a paper slip in front of the chef so he can cook what's been ordered. As everyone knows, this leaves open a reasonable chance for error for each order due to mistakes by the server incorrectly writing down an order, incorrectly recalling it from memory, or illegibly writing an order - leading to misinterpretations by the chef. Empowering the wait staff with Windows Mobile devices would allow them to take orders by making selection from combo boxes rather than writing them out. Orders would instantly stream in from the customer's table to the kitchen, via Merge Replication, where it would be accurately displayed for the chefs.

- **Device Management**
  Lack of device management is the number one pain point for organizations choosing to roll out mobile devices. When an enterprise needs to push out a thousand copies of a mobile line of business application, ActiveSync and a cradle is not a good option. Mobile application binaries can be converted to byte arrays, inserted into SQL Server image columns, and then replicated out to devices over-

the-air where the byte arrays will be rehydrated back into executables and libraries. Devices can report their current health status via Merge by inserting information (such as current battery life, remaining memory, IP address, and the list of installed applications, along with other items) into a local SSCE database and then synchronizing.

Basically, any scenario where data needs to be received, captured or shared is a good candidate for using laptops, tablets, Windows Mobile devices, SSCE and Merge Replication with SQL Server. Instead of the field worker having to wait to return to her office to enter a day's worth of collected data in "batch" mode, she can make her organization more agile and efficient by replicating that data back to her office as it's captured in near real-time.

Running a Magazine

The magazine metaphor might sound like a strange way to describe Merge Replication, but you'll soon see that it's right on the money. I will run you through the discrete pieces that make up the Merge puzzle so you can better visualize how it all works:

- **Publisher**
  The Publisher is the SQL Server that contains the parent database you want to make available to your mobile workforce.

- **Publication**
  The Publication is the actual database you are making available. You can choose to make some, or all, of this database available. Due to this granularity, a Publication is considered a collection of one or more Articles - from the parent database - that runs on the Publisher.

- **Article**
  An Article is a database object that is included in a Publication. These objects can only be tables when synchronizing with SSCE since it doesn't support user-defined views or stored procedures and triggers. So for our purposes, Articles are the Tables you want to replicate down to the mobile database running on SSCE.

- **Distributor**
  The Distributor is a SQL Server that contains the Distribution database. This database stores metadata, snapshots, and status data and is responsible for synchronizing data between the Publisher and Subscribers. The Distributor often resides on the Publisher, but it can

also run on its own server for increased scalability. Think of the Distributor as extra plumbing.

- **Subscriber**
  The Subscriber is the SSCE database running on a laptop, tablet, Windows phone or even another server which is interested in receiving data from the Publisher. The SSCE Client Agent resides at the Subscriber and handles all interaction between the local database engine and the SSCE Server Agent running on IIS. The local database engine keeps track of all the inserts, updates and deletes that are made on the device so it can send those changes to SQL Server during the next sync. SQL Server 2008 can also be a Subscriber by directly connecting with the Publisher via the binary Merge Replication protocol, which is very fast and efficient. Having a full SQL Server Subscriber on another server, or in another data center, is a great way to add disaster-recovery capabilities to your system.

- **Subscription**
  A Subscription is the Subscriber's request for a copy of the Publication. That copy consists of the Articles or Tables that are downloaded and created in SSCE. You also get the table indexes, constraints, referential integrity and, of course, the data. The initial copy is downloaded from the Distributor and is called the Snapshot. Large databases can be downloaded to Windows Mobile devices with very little free RAM due to the fact that the data is parceled out to the device in very small blocks. Keep in mind that SQL Server 2008 can have Subscriptions, as well. Unlike SSCE, SQL Server supports Push Subscriptions.

- **Server Agent**

  The only important element which doesn't fit neatly into the magazine metaphor is how IIS and the SSCE Server Agent work together to provide HTTP(S) access to all the Subscribers. The SSCE Server Agent, which is an ISAPI DLL, the SSCE Replication Provider and the SQL Server Reconciler are collectively known as the SSCE Server Tools and reside on IIS to provide a secure Internet/Intranet gateway between your devices and SQL Server.

- **Republisher**

  A Republisher is a special type of Subscriber, running on SQL Server, with a Subscription to a Publication that's running on a parent SQL Server. It then publishes its Subscription in order to make its data available to Subscribers beneath it. Sounds redundant, doesn't it? While not always necessary, Republishing is Merge Replication's way of scaling-out SQL Server, since a single server can support only a finite number of Subscribers. Just imagine a SQL Server at the top of a pyramid that contains all the data your entire sales force needs. Since your sales force of 100,000 professionals is divided across different geographies, individual sales people only need to synchronize with data that's pertinent to their particular region. Therefore, multiple Republishing SQL Servers containing only filtered, regional data are positioned beneath the top of the pyramid. Instead of overloading the Publisher at the top of the pyramid, regional sales people synchronize with their particular regional Republisher. The takeaway here is to use Republishing whenever you need to scale beyond the capabilities of a single SQL Server.

In the logical architecture diagram shown in Figure 1|1 on the next page, you can see how the Publisher, Distributor, IIS and Subscriber all fit together. You'll notice numerous moving parts on each tier of the architecture, including several Agents designed to do the heavy lifting. I don't suppose this looks like any magazine you've ever heard of.

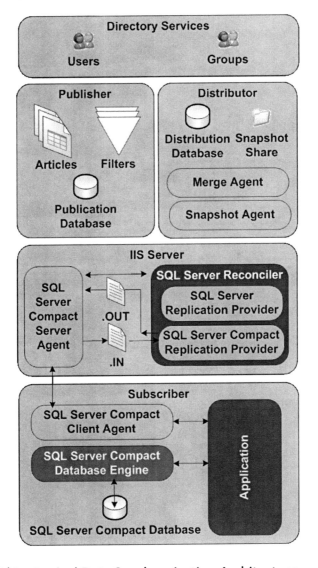

Figure 1|1 > Logical Data Synchronization Architecture

If I translate Figure 1|1 to a physical architecture, like the one shown in Figure 1|2 below, you'll finally see my blueprint for this book. From here on, I am going to teach you how to build a secure, performant and scalable N-Tier Merge Replication architecture that looks much like Figure 1|2. Since SSCE runs almost anywhere, the client endpoint can easily be a Windows phone, a Windows 7 Netbook, a Windows Vista desktop, an Ultramobile PC or even a Tablet PC.

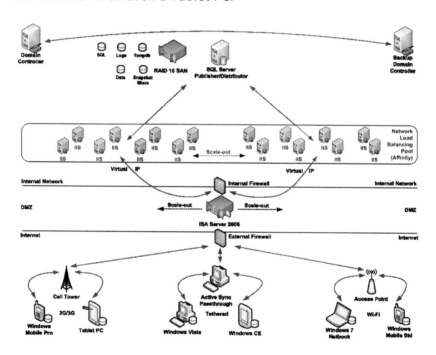

Figure 1|2 > Physical Data Synchronization Architecture

Implementing the Blueprint

The combination of the logical and physical architecture diagrams, plus the deep dives I'm going to take you on in the upcoming chapters, will equip you to build a mobile data synchronization system that will satisfy the needs of the world's largest organizations. Rather than a mere academic exercise, you will find this book to be a hands-on training manual. I won't waste your time with mere theories and concepts, so get ready to roll up your sleeves.

In order to create this book and give you a completely accurate view of how to deploy this system in a large enterprise, I built a private network consisting of a Domain called SYNCDOMAIN, a Domain Controller called SYNCAD, an IIS server called SYNCWEB, and a combined SQL Server Publisher/Distributor called SYNCPUBLISHER. You will see these names used over and over again throughout the book. When you're ready, I'll expect you to piece together your own network, Domain and servers. If you're lacking in the hardware department, you can recreate everything I'm going to teach you on your laptop or desktop through the use of virtual machines running in Hyper-V, Virtual PC 2007 SP1 or Virtual Server 2005 R2 SP1. That's what I did, as I'm running all three servers on my Vista laptop. I added the Microsoft Loopback adapter so that my desktop, device emulators and all three servers can see each other on their own network. You may have even seen this demo at an event like Tech Ed in North America or Europe.

To give what you're doing more context, you'll actually be solving a problem for a hypothetical company called Contoso Bottling. It sells soft drinks through a combination of geographically-dispersed Distribution Centers that maintain inventory, as well as trucks delivering to customers located along their Routes. So we have Inventory, Customers, Distribution Centers, Trucks, Routes and Orders as shown in Figure 1|3.

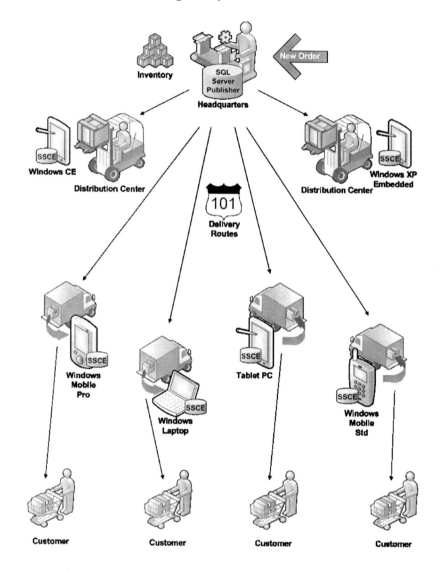

Figure 1|3 > Shipping Orders to Customers

In **Chapter 2**, I'm going to have you create a Domain user and group, which you will configure with appropriate Domain and local permissions. You'll use this Domain group as a security container for all the mobile users to whom you're granting replication access.

In **Chapter 3**, you will create and populate a SQL Server database. This database will be used to illustrate various examples throughout the book. If you've ever used the Microsoft Windows Mobile Line of Business Accelerator that I created, the database should look familiar to you.

In **Chapter 4**, I'll walk you through the configuration of the Distributor tier of the system, which can be combined with the Publisher or set up on a separate server. I will begin by having you create and secure the Snapshot share. You will then move on to the **Configure Distribution Wizard,** where you'll create and secure the Distribution database. I'll also show you how to completely disable distribution and publishing. I'll wrap up the chapter with some ongoing maintenance tips and commentary on how to improve the performance of your Distributor server.

In **Chapter 5**, I'll walk you through the creation of the Publication. This is where you'll make the Contoso Bottling database available to Distribution Centers and route drivers. You'll follow along through the **New Publication Wizard** where you'll learn about Articles and conflict resolvers, as well as Static and Parameterized filters to reduce the amount of data you send to Subscribers.

Chapter 6 picks up where Chapter 5 left off and takes you on a deep dive of configuring the Publisher. I will show you all the best practices needed to make the heart of your Merge Replication infrastructure perform at its very best. I'll also demonstrate tools that allow you to monitor many aspects of replication in real-time so you can quickly identify and troubleshoot any problems that might crop up. I'll finish the chapter with tips on maintaining your Publication database.

Chapter 7 takes you over to the IIS middleware tier of the system, where you get to install the SQL Server Client Components as well as the SSCE Server Tools. I'll then take you on a trip through the **Configure Web Synchronization Wizard,** where you'll create and secure Virtual Directories for use by the SSCE Server Agent. Finally, I'll show you how to tweak your web server to get better performance and scalability.

Chapter 8 tackles the Subscriber tier of the system where developers get to code with C# and the .NET Framework (both big and Compact). In this chapter, I'll show you how to kick off data synchronization sessions from your laptop, tablet or Windows Mobile device by setting properties and calling methods of the SqlCeReplication object. I'll also pass on some tips and tricks I've learned to make sync operations more resilient to network dropouts and other failures.

Summary

This chapter began by laying out the value proposition of the occasionally-connected mobile worker whose mail is facilitated by Exchange Server and data by SQL Server. Unlike many newcomers to the sync space, Merge Replication is a mature technology that has been in use since 1995. The various-use cases illustrate several compelling scenarios designed to add value and bring an ROI to your organization.

Keep in mind that this book specifically covers SQL Server 2008 running on Windows Server 2008 with SQL Server Compact 3.5 SP1 as the mobile client database.

So now that you know what is around the corner in future chapters, let's get started with the tasks I've laid out for you, so you can start helping your customers - or your own organization - get mobilized.

Chapter 2 > Domain Users and Groups

Security First

When it comes to securing a Merge Replication infrastructure, there are a number of paths you can take, ranging from really bad, to bad, to good. It's important to know that IIS and SQL Server can be secured differently from each other.

On your IIS Server where the SSCE Server Agent resides, you can leave things wide open by setting the security to Anonymous. This is how a public web site on the Internet would be configured and is definitely a security "worst" practice. Time and again, I see organizations using this configuration in order to "just get the system running" in a test environment. Unfortunately, this open door to unauthorized Subscribers and hackers often makes its way to production. Other methods of securing IIS include using a local account or utilizing a single Domain user account for all synchronizing Subscribers. These are less-bad, but not optimal, and will not only box you in when it comes to user flexibility, but also leave your environment open to attack when someone figures out what the shared user account is.

On the SQL Server side of things, you can either use SQL Server security or NT security. SQL Server security allows you to create Logins and give them rights to access the database. It also lets you employ the infamous "SA" account with or without a password. This would also be considered a security "worst" practice.

Fortunately, Merge Replication takes advantage of the security services provided by your network's Active Directory. The .NET code on your laptop or device sends the Domain, user name, and password credentials when it synchronizes data. These credentials are used by IIS and SQL Server, which verify them against a Domain Controller. Therefore, the security "best" practice would be to create Domain users and groups that are allowed to participate in the replication of data between SQL Server and SQL Server Compact. To get started, log on to your Windows Server 2008 Domain Controller and from the Start menu, select **All Programs | Administrative Tools**, and click on **Active Directory Users and Computers,** as shown in Figure 2|1.

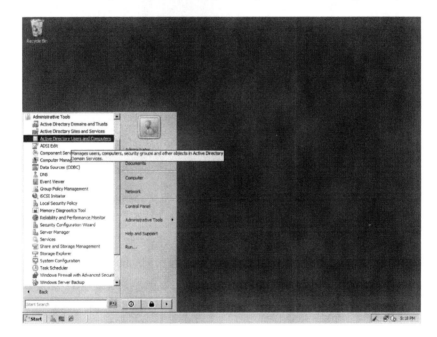

Figure 2|1 > Active Directory Computers and Users

When the **Active Directory Users and Computers** dialog opens, expand the **syncdomain.internal** node and select the **Computers** node to verify that **SYNCPUBLISHER** and **SYNCWEB** are all listed as members of the Domain, as shown in Figure 2|2.

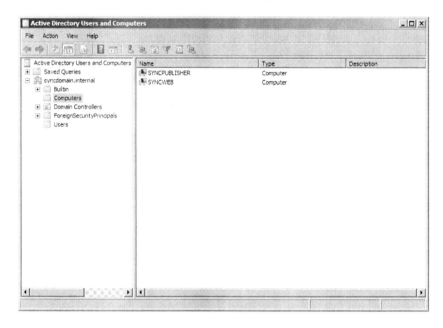

Figure 2|2 > Computers

Whether you've built a real network of servers or you've got everything running in virtual machines, it's important that Active Directory (AD) knows about them and that they can all see each other. Pinging goes a long way in this department. Since you're running Windows Server 2008, the ability to respond to Pings is turned off by default and will need to be manually allowed, via Windows Firewall.

Create a Domain User

Now you need to create a special-purpose user whose credentials will be utilized in your replication environment. Skip down and highlight the **Users** node. Right click on the **Users** node and select **New| User,** as shown in Figure 2|3.

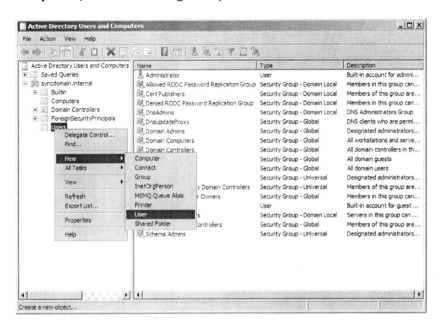

Figure 2|3 > Select New User

This will bring up the **New Object – User** dialog. Enter **Sync** in the
First name text box, **User** in the **Last name** text box, and **SyncUser**
in the **User logon name** text box, as shown in Figure 2|4, and click
Next.

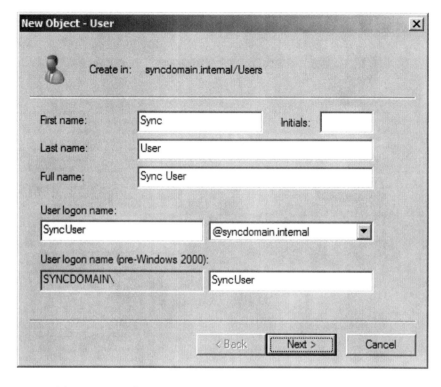

Figure 2|4 > New Object - User

In the next **New Object – User** dialog that appears, enter **P@ssw0rd** in both the **Password** and **Confirm password** text boxes, as shown in Figure 2|5. Ensure that only the **Password never expires** check box is checked and click **Next**.

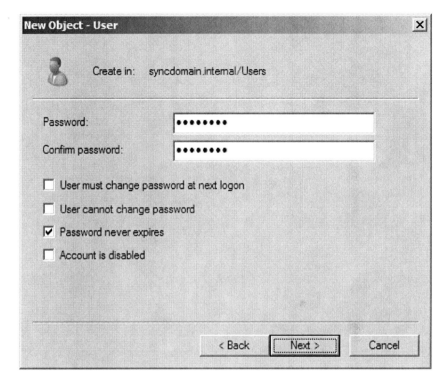

Figure 2|5 > New Object – User Password

The last **New Object – User** dialog will appear and display a summary of your choices, as shown in Figure 2|6. Ensure that they are correct and click **Finish**. You may now close the **Active Directory Users and Computers** dialog.

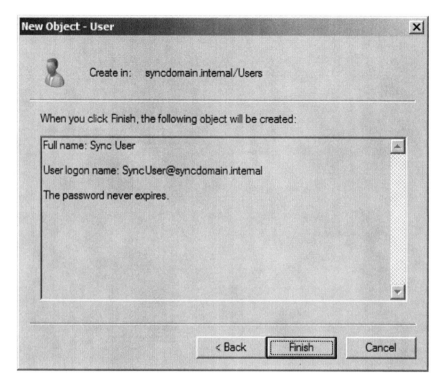

Figure 2|6 > New Object – User

Create a Domain Group

Now it's time to create a Domain-wide group to contain all of the users you want to synchronize. You'll find that creating a group to hold all your mobile users is much easier than adding one user at a time to the SQL Server Logins. Right click on the **Users** node and select **New| Group,** as shown in Figure 2|7.

Figure 2|7 > Select New Group

This will bring up the **New Object – Group** dialog. Enter
SyncGroup in the **Group name** text box, select **Global** for **Group
scope** and **Security** for **Group type,** as shown in Figure 2|8, and
click **OK**.

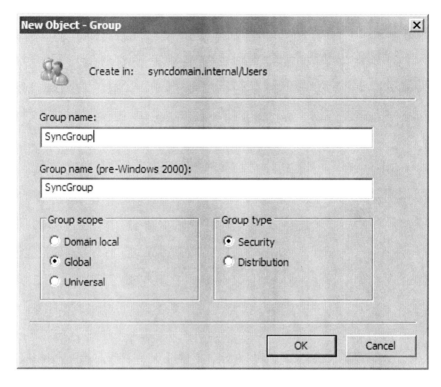

Figure 2|8 > New Object - Group

In order to add your **SyncUser** to the **SyncGroup**, double-click on **SyncGroup** and select the **Members** tab in the **SyncGroup** Properties dialog. Click **Add** to bring up the **Select Users, Contacts, Computers, or Groups** dialog. Type in **SyncUser** and click **Check Names,** as shown in Figure 2|9, and then click **OK** twice.

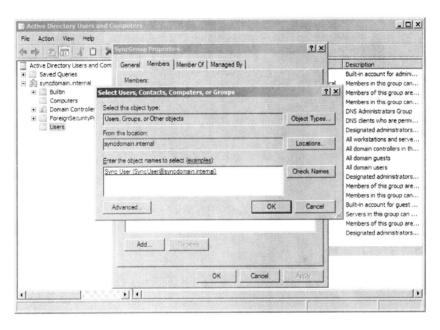

Figure 2|9 > Add SyncUser to SyncGroup

Summary

This will give you everything you need to make it through all of the examples shown in this book. When you're ready to take your system live in production, just add users to your group to allow them to replicate with SQL Server and IIS, via the process described above. Likewise, you can easily revoke a user's synchronization rights by removing them from the sync group.

Using Domain users and groups is a security "best " practice and is preferable to using SA with no password for SQL Server or allowing Anonymous access for your IIS server.

Chapter 3 > Publication Database

Database Schema

Throughout this book, you'll be utilizing a simple supply-chain database called Contoso Bottling, which is designed to help illustrate different aspects of Merge Replication. If you've ever worked with the Microsoft Mobile Line of Business Accelerator, Figure 3|1 below should look familiar.

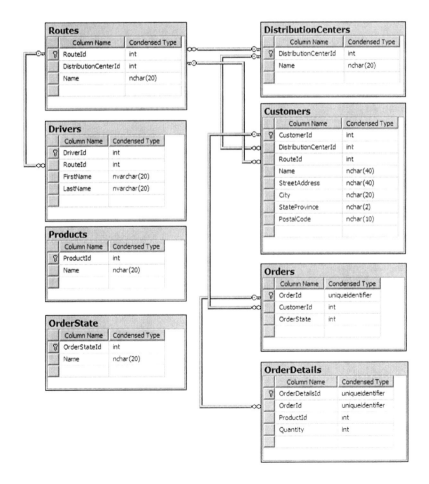

Figure 3|1 > Contoso Bottling schema

In teaching you how to get up and running with Merge Replication, I think it's important to do so in the context of a real solution that you can implement for yourself. That's why I'm giving you a working supply-chain database, modeling the operations of a bottling company. At the highest level, you have Distribution Centers that contain Routes and Customers. Routes also have Drivers, while Customers have Orders and Order Details.

In most industries, Distribution Centers are geographically located near customers as a place to stage inventory for easy delivery. Since everything belongs to the Distribution Centers, this is a logical place to filter if you want to implement Merge Replication Republishing. As shown in the Distribution Centers lookup table in Figure 3|2 below, there's a Distribution Center in both Seattle and Redmond.

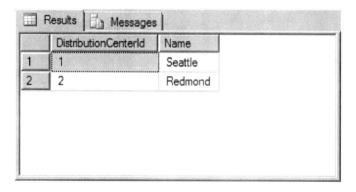

Figure 3|2 > Distribution Centers

The Routes lookup table, shown in Figure 3|3 below, lists the names of the Routes belonging to the Seattle and Redmond Distribution Centers.

	RouteId	DistributionCenterId	Name
1	1	1	Magnolia
2	2	1	Ballard
3	3	1	Fremont
4	4	1	Wallingford
5	5	2	Kirkland
6	6	2	Bellevue
7	7	2	Issaquah
8	8	2	Sammamish

Figure 3|3 > Routes

The Customers lookup table, in Figure 3|4 below, displays a list of Customers and the Distribution Centers and Routes they belong to, respectively. I could have required you to know the Route in order to find the Customers, but as you can see, I've de-normalized the table to improve filter performance and flexibility.

	CustomerId	DistributionCenterId	RouteId	Name	StreetAddress	City	StateProvince	PostalCode
1	1	2	5	A. Datum Corporation	123 Elm	Kirkland	WA	98123
2	2	1	4	Adventure Works LLC	456 Oak	Seattle	WA	98456
3	3	2	6	Fabrikam Inc.	789 Pine	Bellevue	WA	98789
4	4	1	1	City Power & Light	321 Maple	Seattle	WA	98321

Figure 3|4 > Customers

The Drivers lookup table, shown in Figure 3|5 below, lists the first and last names of all Drivers assigned to a given Route. As you might imagine, they deliver products to Customers belonging to their respective Routes.

	DriverId	RouteId	FirstName	LastName
1	1	1	Rob	Tiffany
2	2	1	Loke Uei	Tan
3	3	2	Dan	Bouie
4	4	2	John	Dietz
5	5	3	Derek	Snyder
6	6	3	Stephen	Tong
7	7	4	Steve	Hegenderfer
8	8	4	Mike	Saffitz
9	9	5	Young	Kim
10	10	5	Michael	Jimenez
11	11	6	Paul	Harris
12	12	6	Todd	Versaw
13	13	7	David	Bottomley
14	14	7	Rabi	Satter
15	15	8	Liam	Cavanagh
16	16	8	Khalid	Siddiqui

Figure 3|5 > Drivers

Speaking of Products, the Products lookup table, shown below in Figure 3|6, lists all of the drinks that Contoso Bottling has for sale. To keep things simple, I've glossed over the issue of unit prices, pieces of inventory, bin locations, etc. There's clearly not any inventory management going on here.

Figure 3|6 > Products

The Order State lookup table, shown in Figure 3|7 below, reveals how simple this supply-chain database really is. You've either Placed an Order or you've Delivered it. I've conveniently left out things like picking items from a bin, staging items with a forklift, or loading items on the truck.

Figure 3|7 > Order State

The Orders table, shown in Figure 3|8 on the next page, is where all of the action is in this database. New Orders are Placed for a given Customer, then Delivered.

The GUID displayed in the OrderId column is your tipoff that I've decided to use the Uniqueidentifier data type as my Primary Key, instead an auto-incrementing Integer. This is a good news/bad news kind scenario. The good news is that SQL Server no longer has to manage the Identity ranges of all your SQL Server Compact Subscribers. This is especially good if you've implemented something complex like Merge Replication Republishing. The bad news is that you're now using a 16-byte wide Primary Key, which won't be quite so fast as an Integer for Join queries. I've found myself on both sides of this debate in the past, but now I'm going to put a stake in the ground and say that I've officially joined the GUID camp when it comes to keeping Primary Keys unique. While SQL Server does a great job of tracking and maintaining Identity ranges, I've seen enough issues in the field to punt on this one. With bigger and more complex replication architectures, keeping Primary Keys globally unique is one thing I want to cross off my list and not leave to chance.

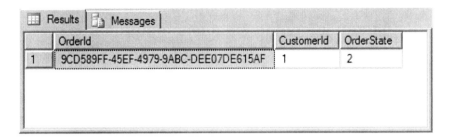

Figure 3|8 > Orders

The Order Details table, shown in Figure 3|9 below, lists which Products - and how many of them - are included for a given Order.

OrderDetailsId	OrderId	ProductId	Quantity
6DFA5659-F2FF-4369-8456-2601B4A9A4AF	9CD589FF-45EF-4979-9ABC-DEE07DE615AF	3	25

Figure 3|9 > Order Details

Create Database

Now that you know what the database looks like, step one in getting the Contoso Bottling database on your SQL Server is to download the zipped-up backup file from the following SkyDrive: http://cid-8b9c82da88af61fc.skydrive.live.com/self.aspx/Public/ContosoBottling.zip.

With the database backup downloaded and unzipped on your server, launch the **SQL Server Management Studio** and connect to the local **Database Engine**. From the Object Explorer, right click on the **Databases** node and select **Restore Database…**, as shown in Figure 3|10.

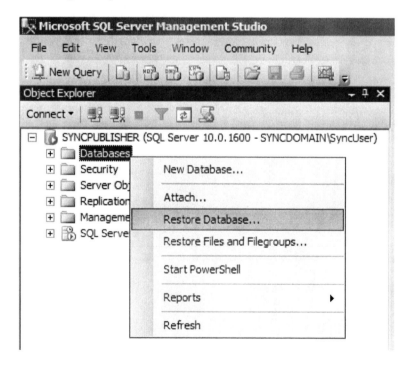

Figure 3|10 > Restore Database

The **Restore Database** dialog will appear, as shown in Figure 3|11. In the **To database** text box, type **ContosoBottling**, skip down and select the **From device** radio button, and then click the ... (ellipsis) button on the right.

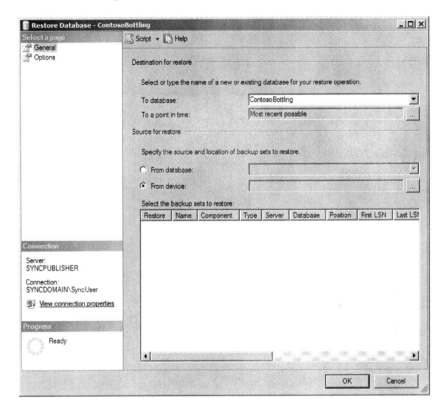

Figure 3|11 > Restore Database - ContosoBottling

The **Specify Backup** dialog will appear, as shown in Figure 3|12. Select **File** from the **Backup media** combo box and then click the **Add** button.

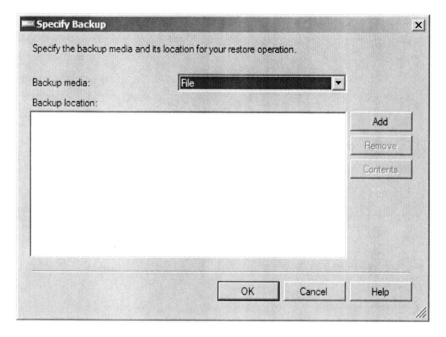

Figure 3|12 > Specify Backup

The **Locate Backup File – SYNCPUBLISHER** dialog will appear defaulted to SQL Server's Backup directory, as shown in Figure 3|13. Navigate to and highlight the **ContosoBottling.bak** file on your server's hard drive and click OK.

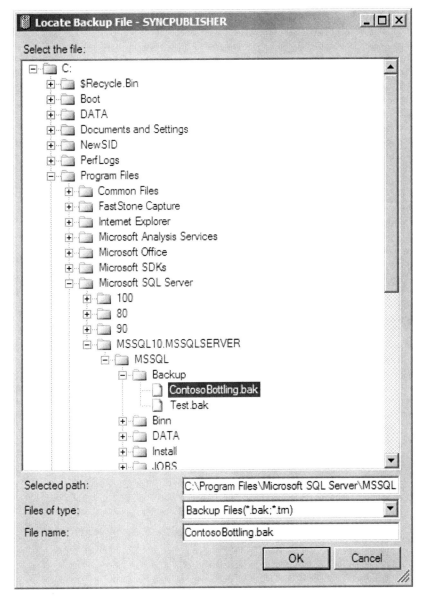

Figure 3|13 > Locate Backup file

You will be returned to the **Specify Backup** dialog. This time, the path to the **ContosoBottling.bak** file will be listed in the **Backup location** list box, as shown in Figure 3|14. Click the **OK** button.

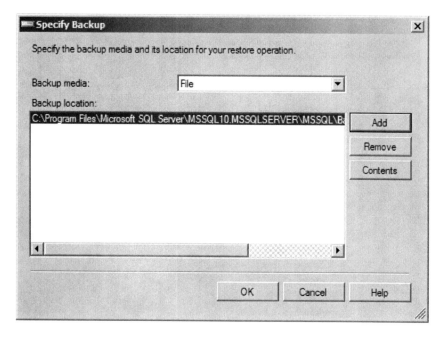

Figure 3|14 > Specify Backup

The **Restore Database – ContosoBottling** dialog now displays your **ContosoBottling** backup in the **Select the backup sets to restore** list view, as shown in Figure 3|15. Select the **Restore** check box.

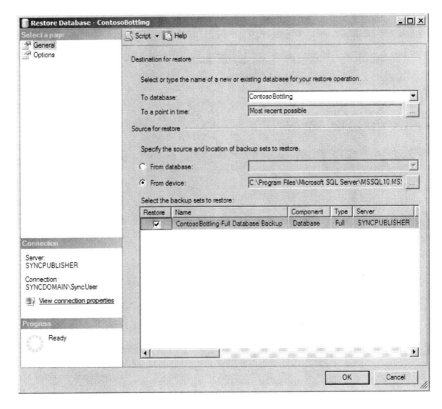

Figure 3|15 > Restore Database General Page

In the **Select a page** section on the left side of the dialog, select **Options**. Check the **Overwrite the existing database** check box, as shown in Figure 3|16, and then navigate to the Restore **the database files as** grid. Once inside the grid, make sure the paths to the database and transaction log files are correct for your server. Keep in mind, when it's time to move your system to production, that for best I/O performance, these two files should be placed on separate, unshared LUNs configured for RAID 10. Click OK to begin the Restore process.

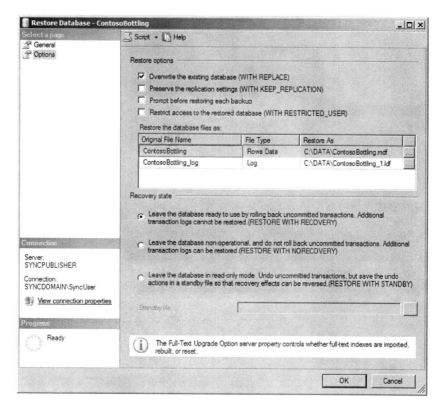

Figure 3|16 > Restore Database Options Page

If everything was configured properly, a dialog saying **The restore of database 'ContosoBottling' completed successfully** will appear, as shown in Figure 3|17.

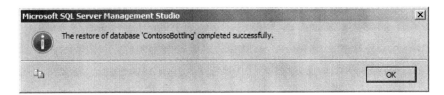

Figure 3|17 > Success

From the **Object Explorer**, expand the **ContosoBottling** node and its **Tables** node to verify that the **Customers, DistributionCenters, Drivers, Orders, OrderDetails, OrderState, Products** and **Routes** tables were created and contain data, as shown in Figure 3|18.

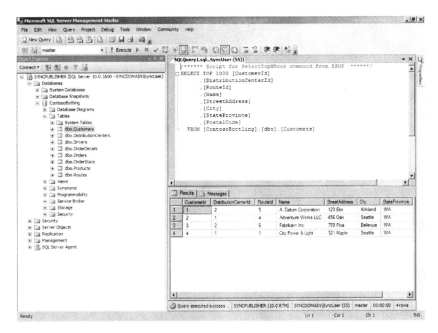

Figure 3|18 > Object Explorer

Summary

I'm hoping that the use of an actual database, as simple as it is, will add a hands-on element to this book aimed at improving your understanding of Merge Replication. This supply-chain database introduces the concept of using GUIDs for Primary Keys instead of auto-incrementing Identity columns to guarantee uniqueness, giving you one less thing to worry about. It illustrates the notion of lookup/reference tables, which you will mark as download-only later in the book. Finally, it foreshadows how you will implement servers-side filtering, based on how Drivers and Customers belong to Routes, Orders belong to Customers, and everything belongs to the Distribution Center.

Chapter 4 > Configuring the Distributor

Chapter Takeaways

The purpose of this chapter is to guide you through the setup and configuration of the SQL Server Distributor tier of this architecture. This server is where you find the Distribution database that's used to store metadata and history data. It's also where database Snapshots reside. The Distributor often runs on the same server as the Publisher, but you do have the option of running it remotely, in order to spread out the load. To keep things simple for the purposes of this book, only a single SQL Server box is needed for both the Publisher and Distributor. You'll get to create and share a folder to hold the database Snapshot files and walk through a wizard that creates the Distribution database for you. You'll also learn how to secure and disable the Distributor, as well as tune your system for performance.

Domain Considerations

The SQL Server tier of the replication environment resides within the corporate network behind your DMZ's back firewall and must be joined to SYNCDOMAIN. Also, the SYNCDOMAIN\syncuser domain user account you created should be added to the local Administrators group on this server, once it's joined to the domain. With this complete, logoff the server and re-logon as SYNCDOMAIN\syncuser to begin installing SQL Server 2008. During the installation, add SYNCDOMAIN\syncuser as your SQL Server administrator on the Database Engine Configuration screen. Clicking **Add Current User** should do the trick.

Create the Snapshot Folder.

One of the duties of the SQL Server Distributor is to host the Snapshot files containing the schema and data from your published tables. It gives IIS Read access to these files via a shared folder you will need to create. From **Windows Explorer**, expand **Computer** and click on Local **Disk (C:).** From the menu, select **File | New | Folder** to create a new folder named **Snapshot**. For best I/O performance, I recommend that you place the Snapshot folder on a disk-drive array other than the one where Windows Server or SQL Server is installed. Optimally, this would be an unshared LUN configured for RAID 10. Right-click **Snapshot** and select **Share,** as shown in Figure 4|1.

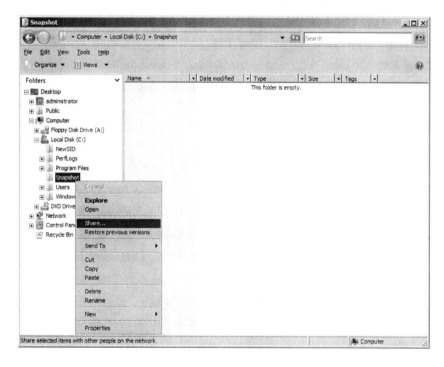

Figure 4|1 > Share Snapshot

In the **File Sharing** dialog box, click the combo box and select **Find…**, as shown in Figure 4|2 below.

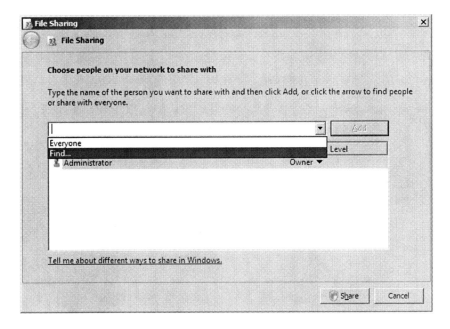

Figure 4|2 > File Sharing Find…

In the **Select Users or Groups** dialog box, click the **Locations** button. In the **Locations** dialog, expand the **Entire Directory** node, select **syncdomain.internal,** and click OK. Type **SyncGroup** in the **Enter the object names to select** text box and click the **Check Names** button, as shown in Figure 4|3. If the user name is confirmed by displaying the full user name, then click **OK**.

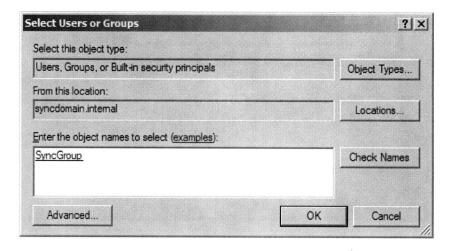

Figure 4|3 > Select Users or Groups

SyncGroup should now be displayed in the list with a permission level of **Reader,** as shown in Figure 4|4.

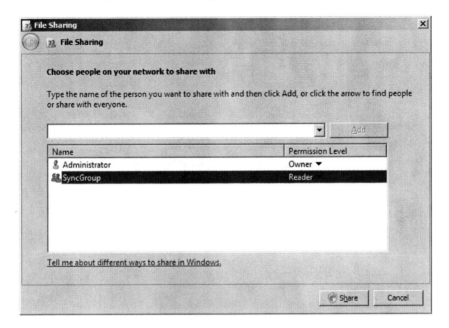

Figure 4|4 > SyncGroup added as Reader

Now you need to further empower your SyncGroup by clicking on it and selecting **Contributor,** as shown in Figure 4|5, so you can write to the share, as well as read from it.

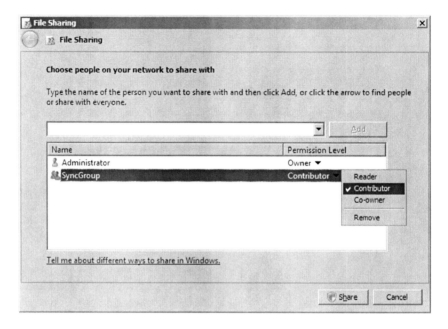

Figure 4|5 > Contributor Permission Level

When you click the **Share** button, the **File Sharing** dialog will update to reflect that the Snapshot folder is now shared, as shown in Figure 4|6 below.

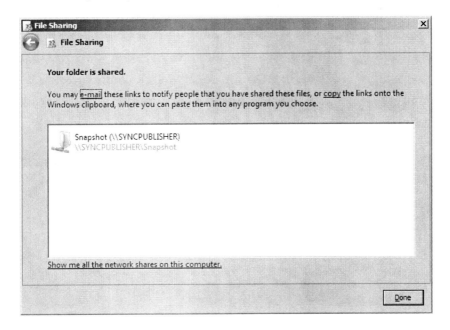

Figure 4|6 > Your folder is shared

Configure Distribution Wizard

Now that you have configured the Snapshot share, it's time to create the Distribution database. From the **Start** menu, select **All Programs | Microsoft SQL Server 2008** and click on **SQL Server Management Studio**. When the **Connect to Server** dialog appears displaying **SYNCPUBLISHER** in the **Server name** combo box, click **Connect**. From the **Object Explorer**, right-click on the **Replication** folder and select **Configure Distribution,** as shown in Figure 4|7.

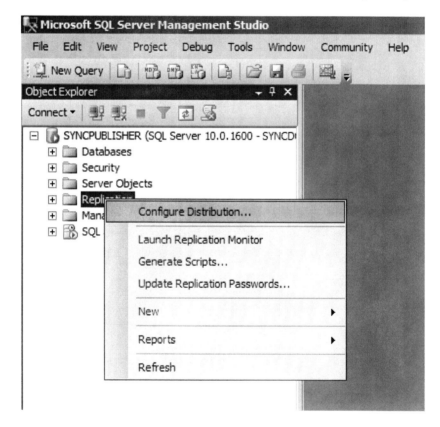

Figure 4|7 > Configure Distribution

The first screen of the **Configure Distribution Wizard** is displayed, as shown in Figure 4|8. Click **Next**.

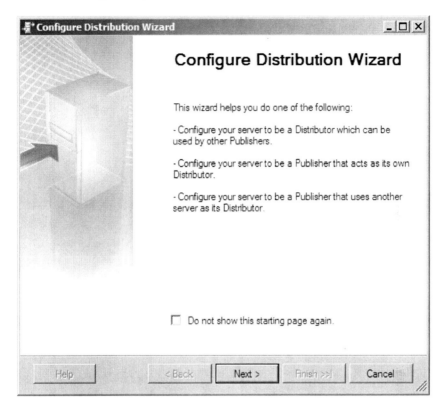

Figure 4|8 > Configure Distribution Wizard

On the **Distributor** screen, shown in 4|9, select the top radio button in order to designate the local server **SYNCPUBLISHER** as the **Distributor**. Click **Next**.

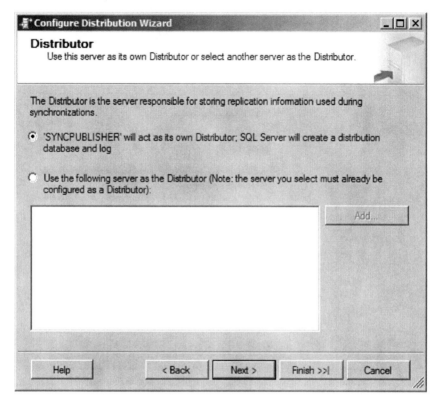

Figure 4|9 > Distributor

On the **Snapshot Folder** screen, shown in Figure 4|10, specify the local server name and Snapshot share you just created in UNC format, then click **Next**.

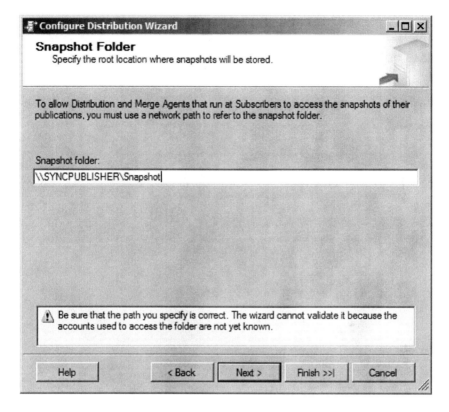

Figure 4|10 > Snapshot Folder

On the **Distribution Database** screen, shown in Figure 4|11, use the default values if you're on a single hard-drive server and then click **Next**. For best I/O performance, I recommend that you specify separate disk drives for both the **Distribution** database and its log file. Not only should those drives be separate from each other, they should also be separate from drives where Windows Server, SQL Server, and the Snapshot share reside. Preferably, they should be on separate, unshared LUNs configured for RAID 10.

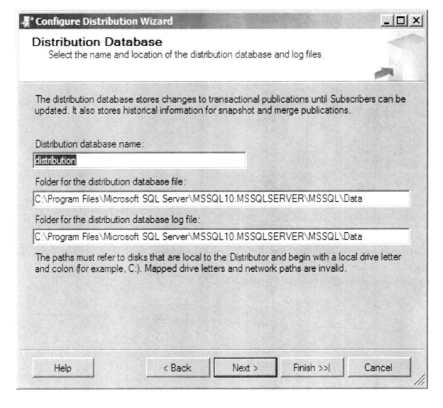

Figure 4|11 > Distribution Database

The **Publishers** screen, shown in Figure 4|12, displays a list of
Publishers configured to communicate with the Distribution
database you are creating. By default, it will show your local SQL
Server. Ensure that **SYNCPUBLISHER** is checked and click **Next**.

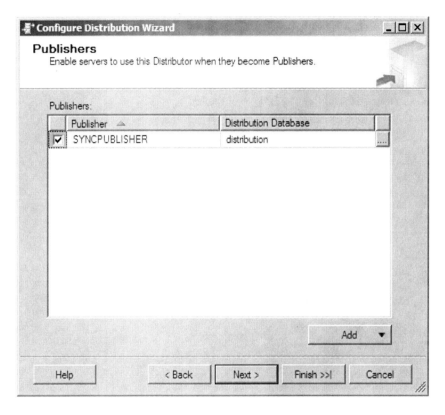

Figure 4|12 > Publishers

The **Wizard Actions** screen, as shown in Figure 4|13, allows you to specify both the configuration of the **Distributor**, as well as the creation of a script file to repeat the process on this server, or any others. Check **Generate a script file with steps to configure distribution** and click **Next**.

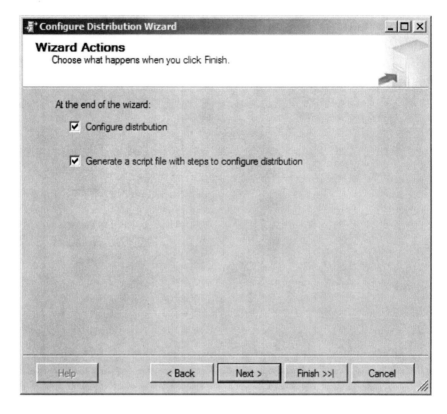

Figure 4|13 > Wizard Actions

Since you chose to create a script file on the previous screen, the **Script File Properties** screen, shown in Figure 4|14, allows you to specify the location of the file. You can also choose whether to append or overwrite the existing script file and choose Unicode or ANSI file formats. Click **Next**.

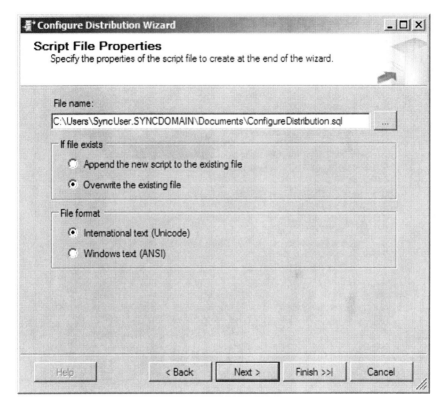

Figure 4|14 > Script File Properties

The **Complete the Wizard** screen, shown in Figure 4|15, provides you with a summary of actions that will occur when you click the **Finish** button. Click **Finish**.

Figure 4|15 > Complete the Wizard

The **Configuring…** screen, shown in Figure 4|16, displays the progress of each of the configuration actions you specified, along with successes, failures, warnings, and descriptive messages. Click **Close** once the actions are completed.

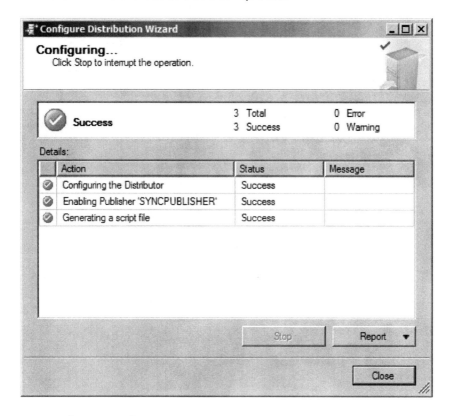

Figure 4|16 > Configuring…

From the **Object Explorer**, expand the **Databases** and **System Databases** folders, as shown in Figure 4|17. If the various Wizard Actions you specified were completed successfully, you should see the newly created **Distribution** database.

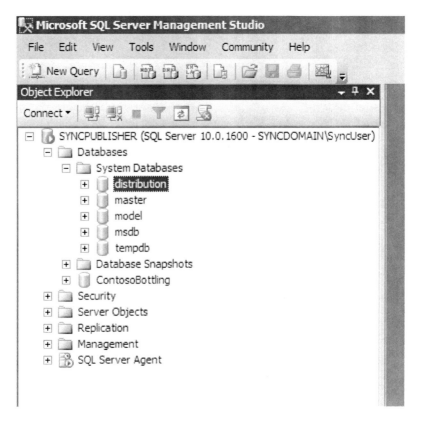

Figure 4|17 > Object Explorer

Securing the Distributor

In order for your Subscribers to communicate with the Distributor, you must first add the appropriate Domain Users or Groups to SQL Server and map them to the Distribution database.

From the **Object Explorer**, expand the **Security** folder and right-click on the **Logins** menu and select **New Login...**, as shown in Figure 4|18.

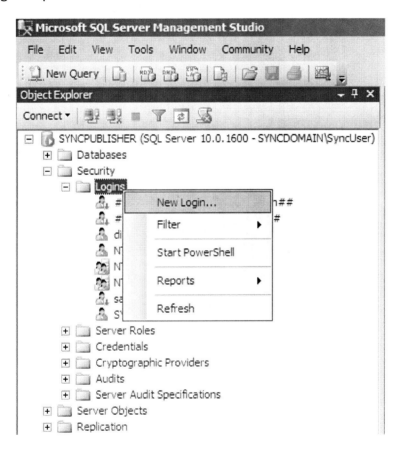

Figure 4|18 > New Login...

In the **Login - New** dialog box, shown in Figure 4|19, select the
Windows Authentication radio button and then click **Search**.

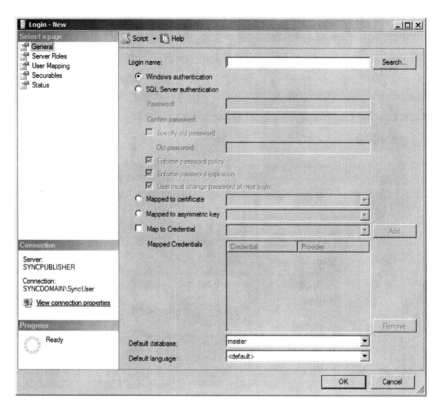

Figure 4|19 > Login - New

In the **Select User or Group** dialog box, shown in Figure 4|20, click the **Locations** button. In the **Locations** dialog, expand the **Entire Directory** node, select **syncdomain.internal** and click **OK**. Type **SyncGroup** in the **Enter the object name to select** text box, then click the **Check Names** button. If the group is confirmed by displaying the full group name then click **OK**.

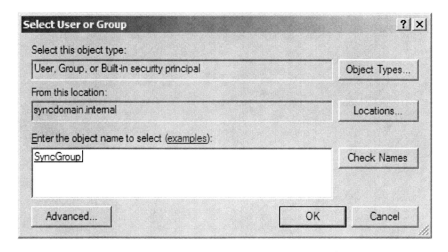

Figure 4|20 > Select User or Group

In the **Select a page** section of the **Login – New** dialog box, click **User Mapping**. From there, check the **Map** check box associated with the **Distribution** database, as shown in Figure 4|21, in order to link the **SyncGroup** credentials and then click **OK**.

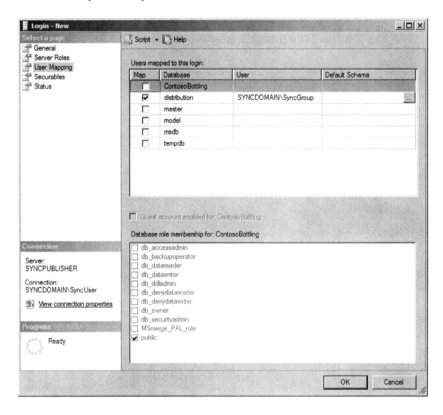

Figure 4|21 > Group Mapping

Disabling a Distributor or Publisher

There may be cases where you will want to remove the Distribution database or delete a Publisher from one or more SQL Servers. Rather than doing all of this manually, there is a wizard that makes it easy to accomplish. From the Object Explorer, right click on the **Replication** folder and select the **Disable Publishing and Distribution** menu, as shown in Figure 4|22.

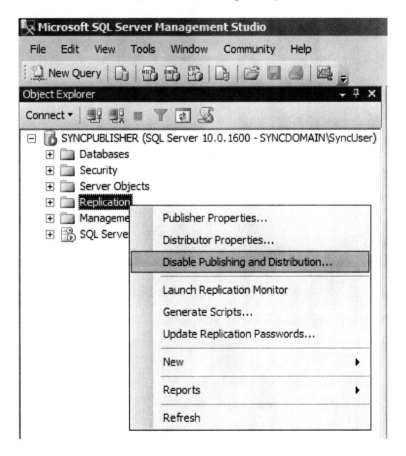

Figure 4|22 > Disable Publishing and Distribution

This first screen of the **Disable Publishing and Distribution Wizard** is displayed in Figure 4|23.

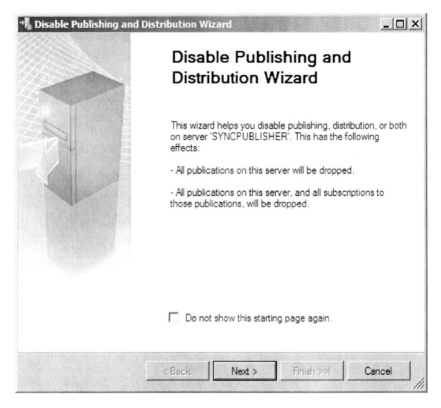

Figure 4|23 > Disable Publishing and Distribution Wizard

On the **Disable Publishing** screen, you should select the **Yes, disable publishing on this server** radio button in order to drop the Distribution database, drop all publications, and drop all subscriptions to a dropped publication, as shown in Figure 4|24.

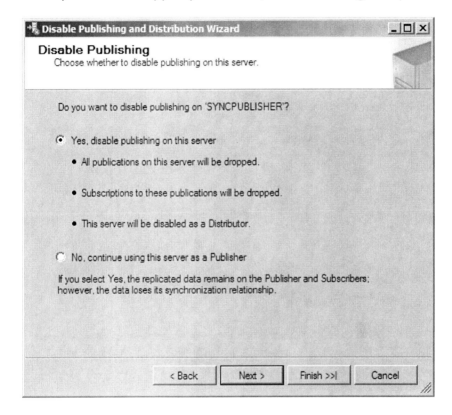

Figure 4|24 > Disable Publishing on this Server

This screen allows you to both disable publishing and distribution, as well as generate a script file in case you want to repeat this process in the future, as shown in Figure 4|25.

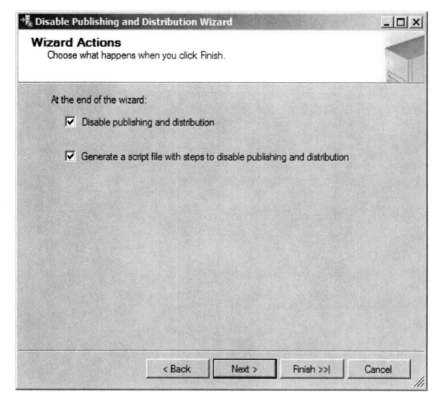

Figure 4|25 > Wizard Actions

If you chose to create a script file on the previous screen, this screen allows you to specify the location of the file. You can choose whether to append or overwrite existing script files and choose Unicode or ANSI file formats, as shown in Figure 4|26.

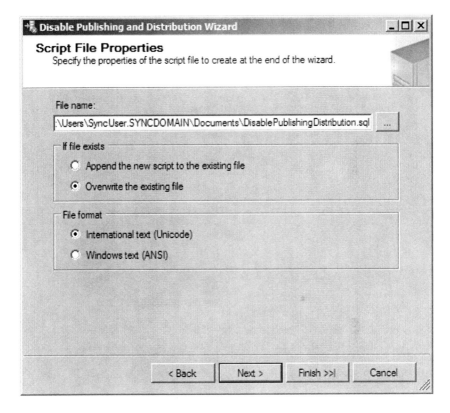

Figure 4|26 > Script File Properties

This screen provides you with a summary of actions that will occur when you click the **Finish** button, as shown in Figure 4|27.

Figure 4|27 > Complete the Wizard

This screen displays the progress of each of the Distribution and Publication actions you specified, along with successes, failures, warnings, and descriptive messages, as shown in Figure 4|28.

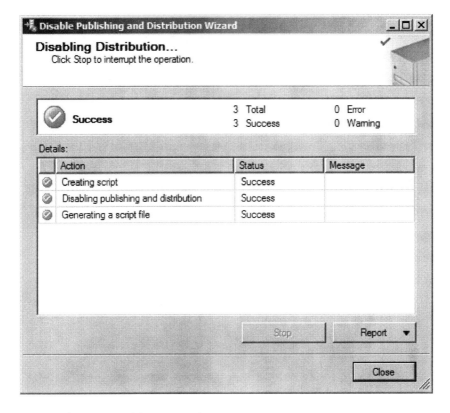

Figure 4|28 > Disabling Distribution...

Performance Tuning

With the Distributor up and running, you can now focus on a couple of performance-tuning opportunities. A big part of how Replication behaves is controlled by the Merge and Snapshot agents that perform much of the heavy lifting. The Snapshot agent is in charge of creating the Snapshot files containing the database schema, table data and other database objects. The Merge agent applies initial Snapshots to Subscriber tables, merges incremental data changes between the Publisher and Subscriber, and reconciles conflicts based on configurable rules. Both of these agents are governed by dozens of parameters that you can configure to boost your system performance. Let me show you how to do this by right clicking on the **Replication** folder and selecting **Distributor Properties,** as shown in Figure 4|29.

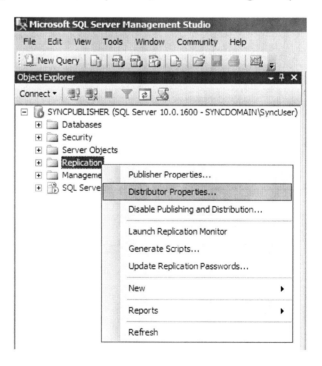

Figure 4|29 > Distributor Properties

From there you'll be presented with the **Distributor Properties –
SYNCPUBLISHER** dialog, as shown in Figure 4|30 below. Click on
the **Profile Defaults** button.

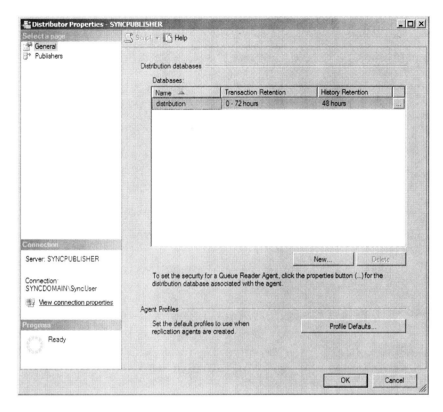

Figure 4|30 > Distributor Properties - SYNCPUBLISHER

This launches the Agent Profiles dialog, where you can see a list of Agents and their respective profiles, as shown in Figure 4|31. In the **Select a page** section of the dialog, I only want you to concern yourself with **Merge Agents** and **Snapshot Agents**. In looking at the figure below with Merge Agent selected, you can see quite a few profiles, reflecting various behaviors for different scenarios.

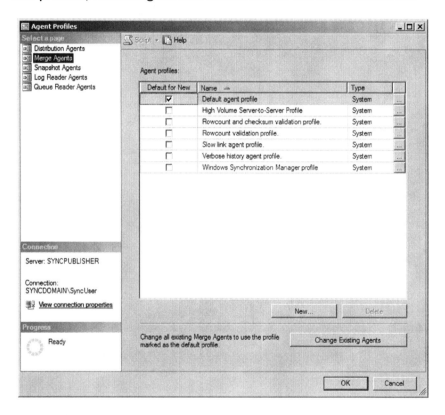

Figure 4|31 > Agent Profiles

The selected **Default agent profile** reflects what I would consider to be a conservative profile designed for slow networks that aren't optimized for performance. Therefore, I want you to create your own Merge Agent profile by clicking the **New** button.

This will bring up the New Agent Profile dialog box, as shown in Figure 4|32.

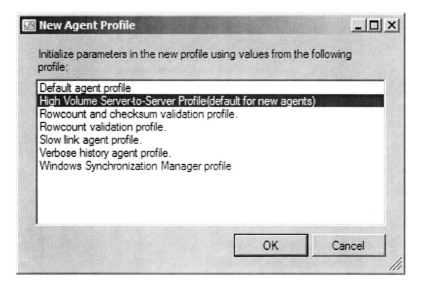

Figure 4|32 > New Agent Profile

Select the **High Volume Server-to-Server** Profile, since I want you to base your new custom profile on this profile, and then click OK.

You'll be presented with a dialog, like the one shown in Figure 4|33, with a blank Name and Description and a very long list of parameter names, default values and current values.

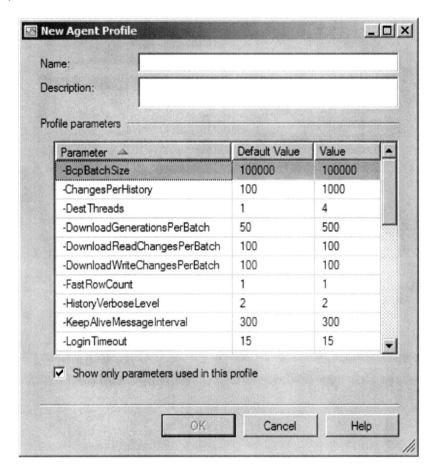

Figure 4|33 > New Agent Profile

I want you to give your profile a name, uncheck the **Show only parameters used in this profile** check box, and stretch out the dialogs so you can see all the different parameters, as I've done in Figure 4|34 below.

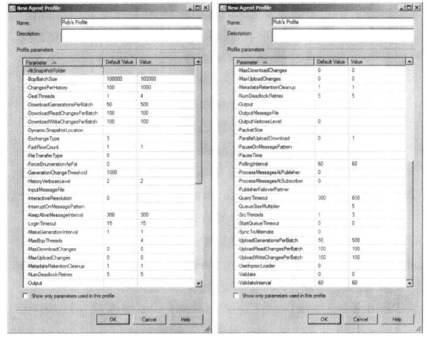

Figure 4|34 > New Agent Profile Parameters

I don't want you to be overwhelmed by the sheer number of parameters, because you only need to concern yourself with a few. Keep in mind that by simply clicking OK to save this new profile, you would instantly have better performance since it's based on the Server-to-Server profile, which does more work per round-trip.

So let's talk about a few parameters that are worth tweaking:

- **DownloadGenerationsPerBatch**: This refers to the number of generations, or rows changed per table since the last sync, that are processed by the Merge Agent as a single batch when downloading changes from the Publisher to the Subscriber. The default value is 50 and the Server-to-Server value is 500. If your network testing confirms that you have a reliable link, you can push up the latter value as high as 2000 to process even more generations per batch.

- **UploadGenerationsPerBatch**: Same commentary as above.

- **HistoryVerboseLevel**: This is all about how much logging happens during replication. The default value is 2, which logs quite a bit of data. Once you feel confident about the stability of your system, you can set this value to 0 to minimize this extra level of I/O going on in your system.

- **MaxBcpThreads**: This value specifies the number of bulk-copy operations that can be performed in parallel. Your new Server-to-Server profile bumps that value to 4, so you should be in good shape as long as your server has enough processor cores to efficiently service these parallel requests while, at the same time, juggling all its other work.

- **ParallelUploadDownload**: This value determines whether or not the Merge Agent will process upload and download changes at the same time. The Server-to-Server profile on which you're basing your new profile enables this functionality and boosts your system performance. That being said, the near-simultaneous calls to certain stored procedures needed to perform a parallel upload and download can also degrade sync performance due to excessive locking and blocking, so don't be afraid to turn this feature off.

- **SrcThreads**: This value specifies how many threads the Merge Agent will use to enumerate changes. Your Server-to-Server value is 3, which should work fine if your system has plenty of free processor cores to work on the task at hand.

This concludes my commentary on Merge Agent parameters, so click **OK** to save and close your new custom profile, which should now appear in your list of Merge Agent profiles.

Now you'll need to repeat this whole process for the Snapshot Agent. Go to the **Select a page** section, highlight **Snapshot Agents**, click the **New** button, and click **OK** on the New Agent Profile dialog box with the Default agent profile selected. You should now be staring at an empty New Agent Profile dialog box, so type in a profile name and uncheck the **Show only parameters used in this profile** check box so it looks like Figure 4|35.

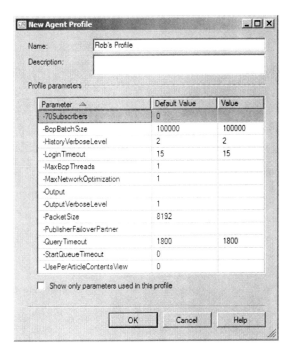

Figure 4|35 > New Agent Profile Parameters

Now we have a new set of parameters to go over:

- **HistoryVerboseLevel**: This works just like the same value with the Merge Agent. When your system is fully debugged, lower this value to 0 to reduce the level of I/O.
- **MaxBcpThreads**: Again, this works the same as with the Merge Agent and is set to 1 by default. If you have the extra processing power, then you can turn it up to help create Snapshot files faster.
- **MaxNetworkOptimization**: This value determines whether or not the system sends lots of potentially irrelevant DELETE commands to all the Subscribers. If your system has multiple partitions where different Subscribers are receiving different sets of data, you should set this value to 1 to reduce the amount of extra network traffic generated by all these DELETE commands being sent out.
- **OutputVerboseLevel**: The value of this parameter determines how much reporting the Snapshot Agent prints out. Its default value is set to 1, but lowering it to 0 will reduce the amount of I/O generated.

Those are the only parameters you need to concern yourself with for the Snapshot Agent, so click **OK** to save and close your new custom profile. It should now appear in your list of Snapshot Agent profiles, so make sure to check it if you want to use it.

Summary

In this chapter, I walked you through the creation of a Snapshot share to hold all your Snapshot files and I showed you how to configure the Distribution database. One point I'd like to emphasize regarding the Snapshot share is: make sure it has a lot of space or the ability to expand, since the number of individual Snapshot folders full of data will grow unabated as you add more Subscribers taking advantage of their own data partitions. Additionally, SQL Server will not delete those folders and files when a Subscription expires, so this is a maintenance task you'll have to take on yourself.

Those of you who have created a Publication before might wonder why I had you create the Distributor separately, when running the Publication wizard does that for you automatically. My reasoning is this: because I want you to have the chance to specify where the Distribution database and transaction log will reside. It's critical that they end up on their own, unshared LUNs configured for RAID 10 when it's time to move your system into production.

In the constant quest for greater performance, I taught you about several Agent parameters you'd probably never heard of. As you crank up the values of some of the parameters I described, I want you to keep one thing in mind: there's no free lunch for many of these parameters if your server doesn't have the processing horsepower and memory to back it all up. Having Agents do more work - and use more threads to accomplish that work - will only pay off if your Windows Server has an extra processor core for each of those threads; this is over and above the cores needed for SQL Server to do the rest of its work. More threads can equal better performance, but it can also mean more work for your system and additional database contention, which leads to locking and blocking. These high-performance settings are great for Republishing between two or more SQL Servers that reside on the same high-speed network in a data center. They may also make good sense in reducing the sync times of your mobile devices, but only if you have a fast, reliable wireless network - which sometimes sounds like an oxymoron. While the default Merge and Snapshot Agent settings may have you scratching your head, those settings might be perfect if your mobile Subscribers have to sync over a slow GPRS network with lots of latency. In some cases, you might need to switch to the Slow link agent profile in order to get Agent settings low enough to support poor performing and highly latent networks. One size does not fit all, so make sure that you thoroughly test all the choices you make before moving them into production.

All right, let's go create the Publication!

Chapter 5 > Creating the Publication

Chapter Takeaways

The purpose of this chapter is to help you turn your Contoso Bottling database into a Publication, via a rather long wizard, so you can share your enterprise data with far-flung laptops, Netbooks and Windows Mobile devices. Along the way, I'll show you how to resolve conflicts and intelligently reduce the amount of data going out to your devices, through a variety of column and row-filtering techniques. I'll even engage in a healthy debate over Identity columns vs. GUIDs, which will definitely keep you on the edge of your seat. While some of the deeper explanations of certain subjects require me to jump off the wizard track from time to time, I assure you that they are completely necessary and I won't keep you derailed for long.

New Publication Wizard

With the SQL Server Distributor configured, it's time to jump over to the server you've designated as the SQL Server Publisher. Before you can make your enterprise data available to your mobile workforce, you must first create a Publication using the longest wizard you've ever encountered. While some of the wizard screens will ask simple questions, others may require you to complete complex tasks. Launch the SQL Server Management Studio so we can get started with the New Publication Wizard.

From the **Object Explorer**, expand the **Replication** folder, right-click on the **Local Publications** folder and select **New Publication**, as shown in Figure 5|1.

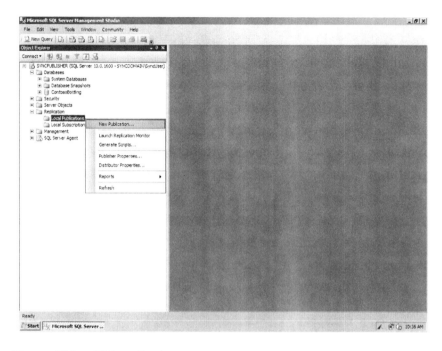

Figure 5|1 > Object Explorer

The first screen of the **New Publication Wizard**, shown in Figure 5|2, is displayed, so click **Next**.

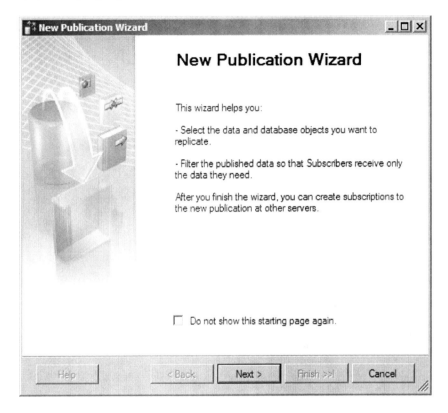

Figure 5|2 > New Publication Wizard

On the **Publication Database** screen, shown in Figure 5|3, select the **ContosoBottling** database from the list of databases and click **Next**.

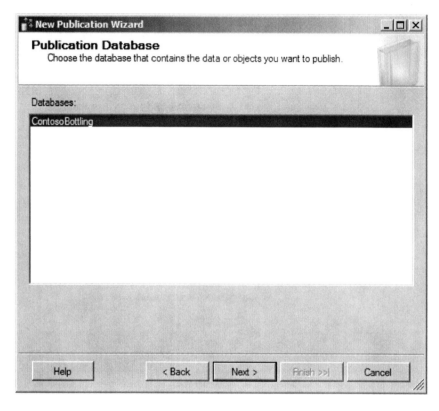

Figure 5|3 > Publication Database

The **Publication Type** screen, shown in Figure 5|4, displays a list of publication types to choose from, based on the needs of your application. Select **Merge publication** from the list and click **Next**.

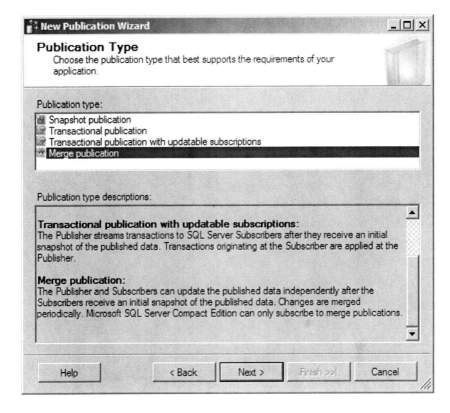

Figure 5|4 > Publication Type

The **Subscriber Types** screen, shown in Figure 5|5, is where you specify which version of SQL Server will subscribe to your publication. Check **SQL Server 2005 Mobile, SQL Server Compact 3.1 and higher** and click **Next**.

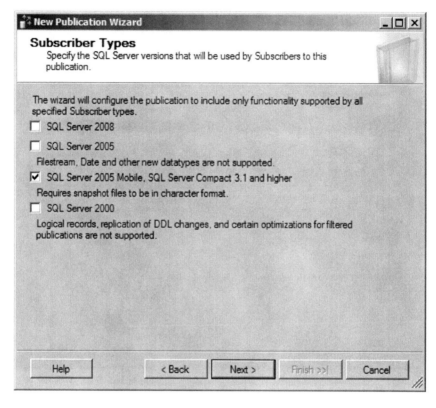

Figure 5|5 > Subscriber Types

The **Articles** screen, shown in Figure 5|6, is where you select the database objects that you want to replicate to SQL Server Compact. Here you see a tree-view of objects to publish, such as **Tables**, **Stored Procedures**, and **User Defined Functions**. Only **Tables** can be replicated to SSCE. Checking **Tables** at the top will ensure that all tables and columns will be published as articles. If your SSCE database doesn't require all the tables or columns found in the publication, you should filter out those objects by un-checking them. This will throttle back your bandwidth requirements, reduce the size of the Snapshot and SSCE database, and ensure that sensitive data doesn't get replicated to the devices.

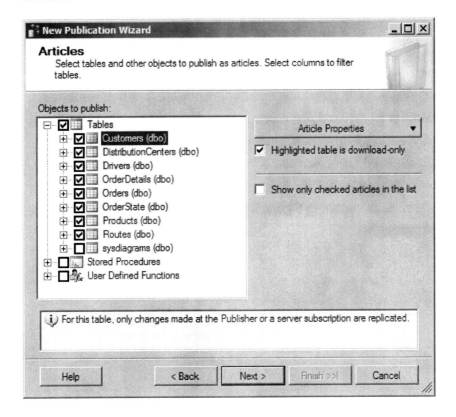

Figure 5|6 > Articles

When you highlight an individual table like the one back in Figure 5|6, you'll notice that a checkbox appears on the right side of the screen, labeled **Highlighted table is download only**. If you check the check box for a given table, it will be marked as download-only meaning that no tracking metadata will be sent to the Subscriber, thereby reducing bandwidth and storage requirements. This tells SQL Server that the Subscriber won't be making changes to the data found in the selected table. Do this for all your lookup/reference tables that your mobile users won't modify, in order to improve performance. Highlight the **Customers, DistributionCenters, Drivers, OrderState, Products** and **Routes** tables and mark each of them as download-only by checking the check box on the right.

When you highlight any of your tables, you also have the ability to click **Article Properties** to set properties for that table. As well, you have the option to set global properties for all of the tables. In order to explore these properties, highlight the **Orders** table, click **Article Properties**, and select **Set Properties of the Highlighted Table Article**. If a **New Publication Wizard** dialog pops up, just click **OK**. The **Article Properties – Orders** dialog appears, as shown in Figure 5|7 on the next page, with a long list of properties.

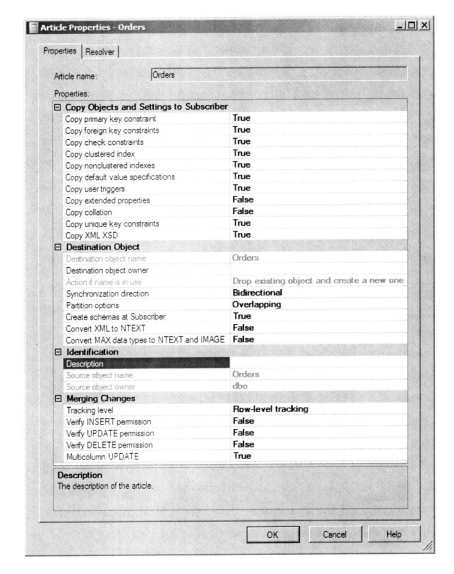

Figure 5|7 > Article Properties – Orders - Properties

Looking from top to bottom, you should see four different sections. It's generally a good idea to leave the settings in the **Copy Objects and Settings to Subscriber** section as is.

In the **Destination Object** section, you might find yourself changing the **Synchronization direction** property. Typically, it's set to **Bidirectional,** which means that data is downloaded and tracked, and all changes are merged back into SQL Server. Other options for this property include **Download-only to Subscriber, prohibit Subscriber changes** and **Download-only to Subscriber, allow Subscriber changes**. You would choose this latter option if you want to allow the Subscriber to add, update or delete data in that reference table without having those changes being tracked or merged back into SQL Server - a private data store for the Subscriber, as it were.

There's really nothing notable in the **Identification** section, so you can skip over it. If you were using an Identity column for your table's Primary key, you would see an **Identity Range Management** section. You don't see one for the Orders table because I chose to use a Uniqueidentifier as my Primary Key. Since many databases utilize auto-incrementing Integer and BigInt columns as unique Primary Keys, there's a danger when replicating out copies of the same database to multiple subscribers: if everyone has the same series of Integers in their Key and they insert a new row into the same table, they will all auto-increment to the same next value in the sequence, but with different data in the new row; when the Subscribers go to merge their changes into SQL Server, they will all have Key collisions and only one Subscriber's insert will be accepted, while all others will be discarded. SQL Server avoids this problem by giving each Subscriber their own range of 1,000 Identity values that are different from the ranges given to the other Subscribers. I might get 1-1,000 and you might get 1,001-2,000. This way, our Keys will never collide. When a Subscriber has used 80 percent of their Identity values, she will be assigned a new block of 1,000 values.

This is definitely a great feature and one less thing for you to worry about. While this sounds cool, it's not completely foolproof. I've seen scenarios where a database ran out of Integers or a device failed to receive a new batch of Identity ranges because it was disconnected for so long. Additionally, Merge Replication had to perform extra work and utilize additional tables to keep track of all of this. If you have a small installation under 1,000 Subscribers and a database that's already using Identity columns, I wouldn't change a thing. On the other hand, if you're deploying to thousands or tens of thousands of Subscribers, you might consider using GUIDs to keep your table's rows globally unique. Keep in mind that SQL Server is already going to add a Uniqueidentifier column to all of your tables for tracking purposes anyway. You can beat SQL Server to the punch by using a Uniqueidentifier column as the Primary Key for all of your tables and setting that column to RowGUID. This way, SQL Server won't add an additional column to your tables and won't have to perform the extra work of tracking Identity ranges. Is there a downside to this? Sure. A Uniqueidentifier represents a 16-byte wide Key, which won't be as fast as a 4-byte wide Integer when it comes to multi-table joins. On the other hand, using GUIDs means you'll never experience things like Key collisions, running out of Integers, or not getting a new batch of Identity ranges. If you find yourself building a very large Merge Replication infrastructure where you need to use Republishing, the use of Identity ranges adds an undesirable level of complexity that will keep you up at night. I've personally decided to go with GUIDs.

If you drop down to the **Merging Changes** section, the first property you'll see is **Tracking level**. By default, this is set to **Row-level tracking** , for which SQL Server is optimized. This means that if any two Subscribers make a change to any column in the same row, the **Merge Agent** treats them as a conflict and launches the conflict resolver specified for the article in question in order to determine a winner. Winning rows are applied to the Publisher and Subscriber, while losing rows are written to the conflict table. If you switch the property to **Column-level tracking**, two Subscribers can make changes to different columns in the same row and the **Merge Agent** will not consider that to be a conflict to resolve. Additionally, it uses significantly less bandwidth than its Row-level counterpart since it sends less information during a synchronization. While this may seem like the way to go, you should use **Column-level tracking** only on tables that absolutely need it, because **Row-level tracking** yields superior synchronization performance on SQL Server due to the fact that additional processing of column metadata isn't required. Keep in mind that **Row-level tracking** maintains its edge over **Column-level tracking** until your tables start to contain image, ntext, binary, or nvarchar(max) typed columns. As with most things associated with Merge Replication, every scenario is different, so test it for yourself.

Looking back at Figure 5|7 from a few pages ago, a click on the **Resolver** tab will reveal a list of conflict resolvers, as shown in Figure 5|8. This collection of rules engines that determine who wins and who loses is a feature you will be hard-pressed to find in any other synchronization technology. You get a default resolver with a rule that says the first change written to the Publisher wins, whether that change was made directly to the Publisher or whether it came from a device. You also have the option of choosing 1 of 12 pre-built resolvers, or you can create your own in .NET or as a stored procedure.

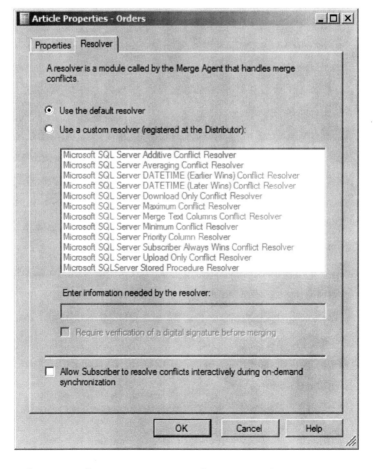

Figure 5|8 > Article Properties – Orders – Resolver

Some notable built-in resolvers you can choose from include:

- DATETIME (Earlier): Must specify a DATETIME column for each table you want to resolve this way. The column with the earlier DATETIME value is the winner. Time zones are not factored in the decision. If one of the values is set to NULL, then it loses.
- DATETIME (Later): Must specify a DATETIME column for each table you want to resolve this way. The column with the later DATETIME value is the winner. Again, time zones are not factored in the decision and if one of the values is set to NULL, then it loses.
- Maximum Conflict: Must specify a numeric column for each table you want to resolve this way. The column with the larger value is the winner. If one of the values is set to NULL, it loses.
- Minimum Conflict: Must specify a numeric column for each table you want to resolve this way. The column with the smaller value is the winner. If one of the values is set to NULL, it loses.
- Subscriber Always Wins: Hmmm... I guess it means that the Subscriber always wins.
- Priority Column: Similar to the Maximum Conflict resolver, but adds support for update conflicts.
- Upload Only: Changes uploaded to the Publisher are accepted.
- Download Only: Changes uploaded to the Publisher are rejected.
- Stored Procedure: A stored procedure with custom conflict resolution logic is called.

Click the **Cancel** button to close the dialog and click **Next**.

The **Article Issues** screen, shown in Figure 5|9, informs you that **Uniqueidentifier columns will be added to your tables**. This happens if you have tables using something other than a GUID with the ROWGUIDCOL property set for a Primary Key. In the case of our ContosoBottling database, I used Integers as Primary Keys for all the download-only lookup tables, since a Subscriber on her Windows 7 Netbook can't change those values and there's no danger of Key collisions. I did, of course, use GUIDs for the Orders and OrderDetail tables, since they are transactional. Click **Next**.

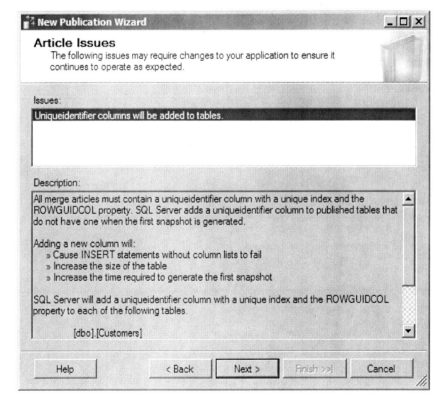

Figure 5|9 > Article Issues

The **Filter Table Rows** screen, shown in Figure 5|10, allows you to filter the rows of the tables you choose to publish as Articles. This is arguably the most powerful feature of Merge Replication. Through the use of graphical tools, you can create server-side business logic that is executed whenever a Subscriber synchronizes. Instead of sending all of the data to everyone, this feature allows you to create:

- Static filters that filter/reduce data going to everyone.
- Parameterized filters that filter/reduce data going to a particular Subscriber, based on a unique variable that's passed to the server by the Subscriber.

Click **Add** and then select **Add Filter** to explore this powerful functionality.

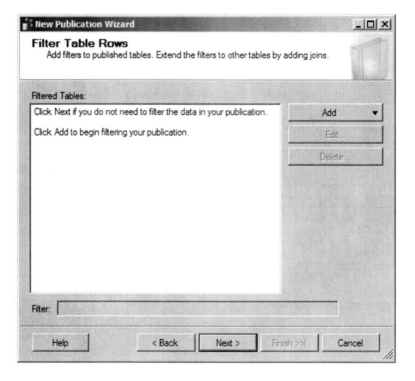

Figure 5|10 > Filter Table Rows

The **Add Filter** dialog box, shown in Figure 5|11, is where you can: first) select a table to filter from the combo box at the top; next) see the table's columns in the **Columns** list box on the left; and finally) complete the WHERE clause of the SQL statement in the **Filter statement** text box on the right. Selecting **Drivers** from the combo box and double-clicking the **LastName** column on the left will move it over to the **Filter statement** on the right. By adding a SQL statement to the WHERE clause, like **LastName = Gates** for instance, you would create a Static Filter where everyone would download a Drivers table with the same **Gates** data. Since we want to retrieve a unique DriverId and RouteId, we will create a Parameterized filter by instead saying **LastName = HOST_NAME()**. A dynamic Subscriber variable is reflected in the SQL Server function called HOST_NAME(). With this particular WHERE clause, you would determine to which RouteId a unique Subscriber (who is a route driver in this scenario) belongs.

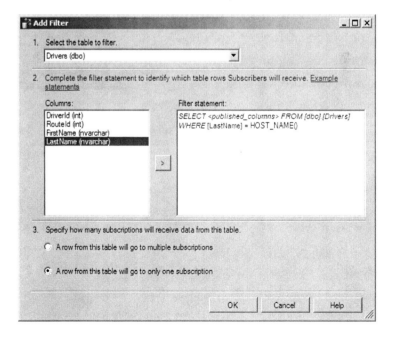

Figure 5|11 > Add Filter

The net result is that different mobile subscribers can receive different subsets of the database without requiring multiple Publications to be created. This can also help to avoid conflicts which could otherwise be caused by multiple mobile subscribers updating the same data.

So you're probably wondering: how can a Subscriber working out in the field send along a value that shows up in the HOST_NAME() function? Lucky for you .NET developers out there, there's an SqlCeReplication object that happens to have a Hostname property that you can set to a string value to send up to SQL Server during a sync. As you might imagine, the column match that you're trying to find for your HOST_NAME() value must use an nchar or nvarchar data type for this to work smoothly, as in our example on the previous page.

For arguments sake, let's say that you want to send up an Employee Id number HOST_NAME() value to match up with an Integer column, instead of a name. On the .NET side, you'd need to surround the Employee Id number in quotes, and on the SQL Server side you need to adjust the text in your filter statement to use the CONVERT() function in the WHERE clause. The new filter that converts an nchar to an integer would look like the following:

```
CONVERT(nchar, integercolumnname) = HOST_NAME()
```

Let's take one more look at the **Add Filter** dialog, shown in Figure 5|11, before moving on. At the bottom of the dialog, you see two radio buttons. Selecting **A row from this table will go to multiple subscriptions** means that more than one Subscriber can send the same HOST_NAME() value, creating an Overlapping Partition. Selecting **A row from this table will go to only one subscription** means that SQL Server will only accept a unique HOST_NAME() value from a single Subscriber, creating a Non-overlapping Partition. If another Subscriber tries to send the same value, an error will occur. If you can guarantee that only one Subscriber will send a unique value, selecting the second option will result in SQL Server giving you better synchronization performance by minimizing the upload cost with Precomputed partitions and reduced use of tracking tables. All Static Filters should select the first radio button since all Subscribers would receive the same set of filtered rows. Click the lower radio button and then click **OK** to take you back to the original **Filter Table Rows** dialog with the **Drivers** table added, as shown in Figure 5|12.

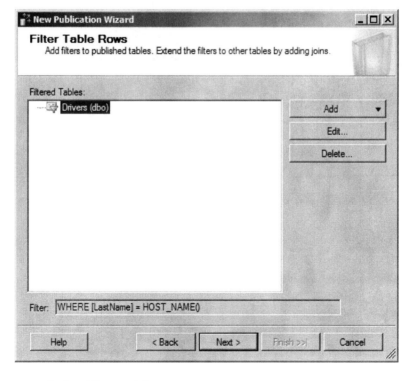

Figure 5|12 > Filter Table Rows

Now, I'm going to show you how to create a Join filter. This allows a child table to be filtered, based on how a parent table is filtered. In our case, the **Drivers** table is dynamically filtered based on the HOST_NAME() value passed to it, which returns a specific DriverId and RouteId to the Subscriber. The Subscriber also wants to see data found in the other tables. Not all the data, just the rows that are meaningful to this particular driver.

To start this process, click on the **Drivers** icon in the **Filtered Tables** list box to highlight it. Click the **Add** button and then select **Add Join to Extend the Selected Filter…**, as shown in Figure 5|13.

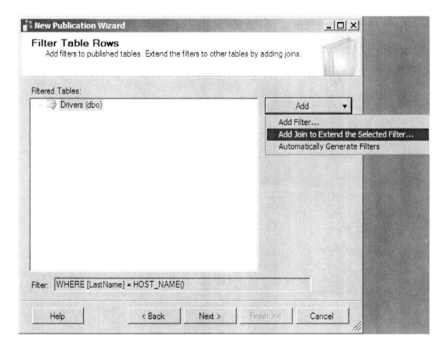

Figure 5|13 > Add Join to Extend the Selected Filter…

The **Add Join** dialog presents you with the steps needed to create the Join filter, as shown in Figure 5|14.

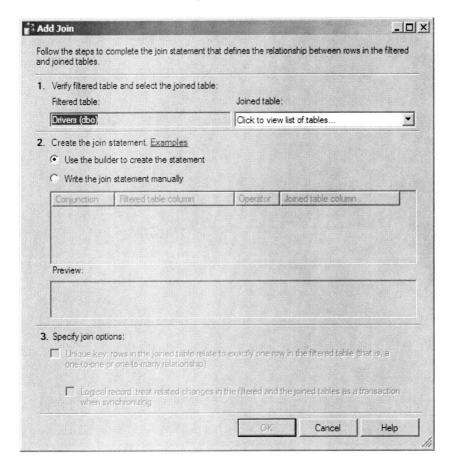

Figure 5|14 > Add Join

Using the tools provided in this dialog, you will be able to join the Primary key of one table to the foreign key of another.

In step 1, verify that the proper **Filtered table** has been selected, as shown in Figure 5|15. In our case, that would be **Drivers**. In the Joined table combo box on the right, select **Routes,** since that's the table to which we want to extend the **Drivers** filter.

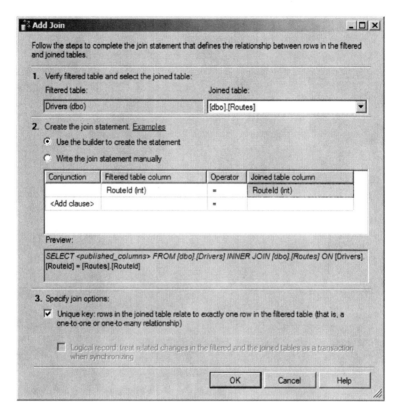

Figure 5|15 > Add Join

In step 2, stick with using the builder and drop down to the list box. The **Filtered table column** represents the Drivers table, so I'd like you click on the row beneath the header and select RouteId. Over to the right, you'll see the **Joined table column** which represents the Routes table. I want you to select RouteId which just so happens to be the Primary Key for the Routes table. As you make your selections, you'll notice an INNER JOIN SQL statement being created in the **Preview** area.

So what just happened here? We know that by sending our driver's last name as the HOST_NAME() filter, we reduced to just one the number of rows returned by the Drivers table. We know that one of those columns gave us a single RouteId value that we could connect to the Routes table. By joining with the RouteId of the Routes table, we only retrieve the rows that are relevant to our driver. Since the two tables were already related to each other via referential integrity, it's possible that the column values are automatically selected for you. Pretty cool.

If you click around the various combo boxes in the join statement builder, you see that you can further filter your results by selecting different columns, operators, and even additional conjunction clauses. You also have the option of creating your join statement by hand, if you wish. Since we have a one-to-one relationship between **Drivers** and **Routes**, check the **Unique key** check box in step 3, so SQL Server can further optimize the Join. Keep in mind, it is imperative that the columns involved in the join should be part of an index that is unique, if at all possible, on both sides of the join to improve performance.

Normally, you might think it's time to move on to the next topic of this book. Since I intend for you to actually build a complete Merge Replication environment, I'm going to have you repeat this Join filter process a few times so that the entire database is filtered in such a way that the Driver gets the right amount of data to do his or her job. Clicking **OK** will return you to the **Filter Table Rows** dialog, from Figure 5|13. Highlight **Drivers** again, click the **Add** button and then select **Add Join to Extend the Selected Filter** for me.

This time I want you to select **Customers** as your Joined table. Just as with the first Join filter you created, I want you to select **RouteId** for both the **Drivers** and **Customers** table and check the **Unique key** check box, as shown in Figure 5|16.

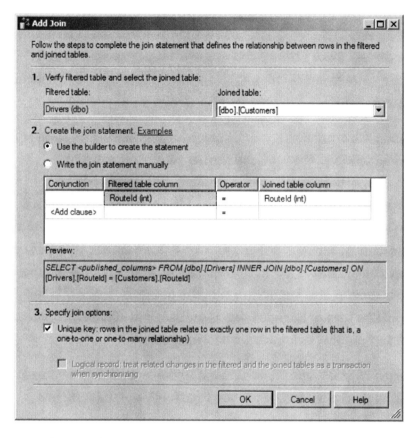

Figure 5|16 > Add Join

As it turns out, just like Drivers, Customers also belong to a specific route. With this filter in place, the Driver only sees the customers who are valid for his or her route, instead of seeing all the customers. Click **OK** to save and to return you to the **Filter Table Rows** dialog. Expand **Drivers** this time, highlight **Customers** and click the **Add** button, and then select **Add Join to Extend the Selected Filter**.

You've now ventured into the territory of creating a Join filter based on a table that has already had its rows reduced by a Join filter. Your driver is only receiving customers that belong to him, and his route. It makes sense that your driver would only like to see the orders that belong to his customers, instead of seeing everyone's orders. This will easily be accomplished by selecting **CustomerId** from both the **Customers** and **Orders** table and checking the **Unique key** check box, as shown in Figure 5|17.

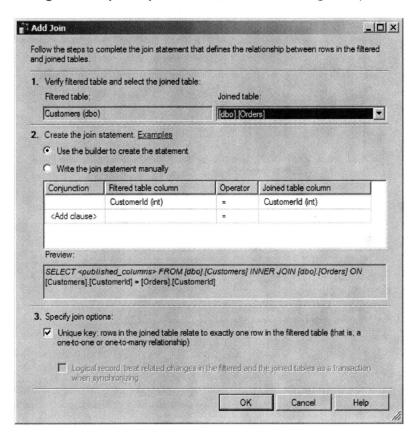

Figure 5|17 > Add Join

Click **OK** to save and to return you to the **Filter Table Rows** dialog. Expand **Customers** this time, highlight **Orders** and click the **Add** button, and then select **Add Join to Extend the Selected Filter**.

Now that your driver is only receiving orders for the customers on his route, let's use the magic of Primary and Foreign Keys, plus referential integrity, to return only the OrderDetails that belong to your driver's orders. Select **OrderId** from both the **Orders** and **OrderDetails** table and check the **Unique key** check box, as shown in Figure 5|18.

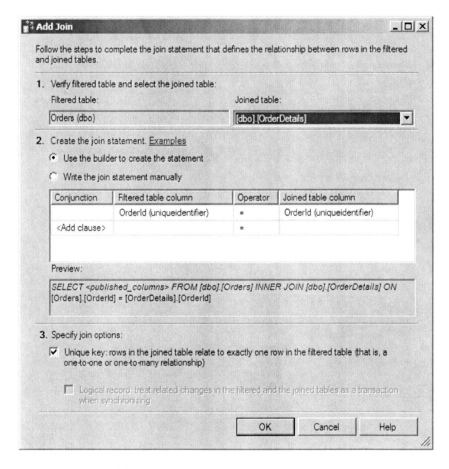

Figure 5|18 > Add Join

Click **OK** to save and to return you to the **Filter Table Rows** dialog. Expand **Drivers**, highlight **Routes** and click the **Add** button, and then select **Add Join to Extend the Selected Filter**.

The last piece of this puzzle is to determine which Distribution
Center the driver belongs to whenever he syncs. Since Routes
belong to Distribution Centers, Customers belong to Routes, and
Orders belong to Customers, you're almost home. Select
DistributionCenterId from both the **Routes** and
DistributionCenters table and check the **Unique key** check box, as
shown in Figure 5|19.

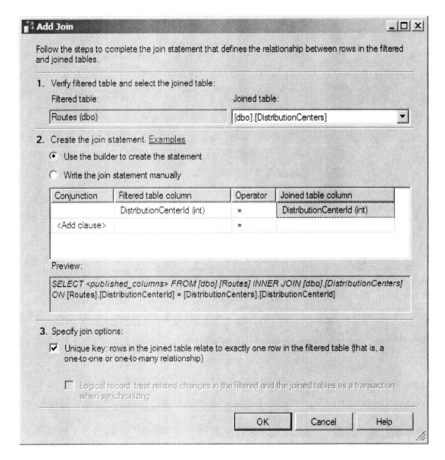

Figure 5|19 > Add Join

When you click **OK** to save this time, you're returned to a **Filter Table Rows** dialog that looks like Figure 5|20 below.

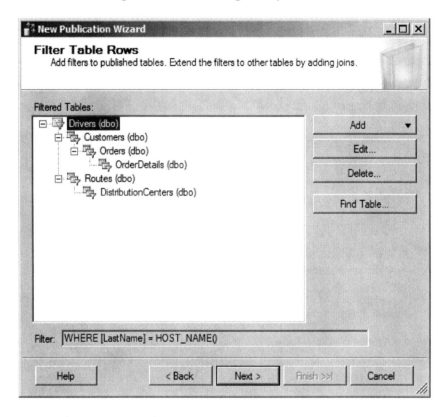

Figure 5|20 > Filter Table Rows

You can see that you've created a nice little hierarchy of filters, ensuring that the right data goes to the right Subscriber. Thanks for putting up with all this monotonous filter creation. Click **Next** to put filter creation in the rear view mirror.

The **Snapshot Agent** screen lets you specify when to create a database Snapshot, as shown in Figure 5|21. Snapshots represent the schema of the database you want to sync with your Subscribers. They are important because whenever a Subscriber performs their first sync, it's the Snapshot that creates the structure of the SSCE database. It's also important to have the Snapshot Agent create new Snapshots often to keep things fresh. Out-of-date Snapshots mean that after a Subscriber has downloaded the initial copy of the database, he'll have to wait a bit longer while SSCE continues to replicate with SQL Server in order for the local database to "catch up" with the current state of the Publication database. Alter how often the **Snapshot Agent** runs by clicking the **Change** button.

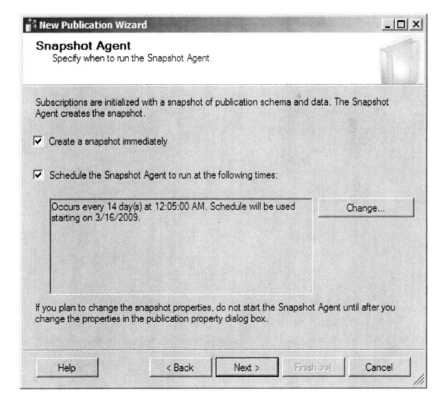

Figure 5|21 > Snapshot Agent

When the **Job Schedule Properties** dialog appears, as shown in Figure 5|22, you'll notice that the default frequency of creating new Snapshots is every 14 days. That happens to be the default number of days an unsynchronized Subscription stays active before expiring. I've already mentioned the importance of keeping Snapshot data fresh and that's why I want you to set recurrence value to every **1** day. You can have this job kick off in the middle of the night to create a fresh new Snapshot, which will ensure that all database initializations and re-initializations happen as fast as possible. The other important reason to create Snapshots every night is to avoid Subscription expiration errors I've seen from time to time as a result of out of date Snapshots. Click **OK**.

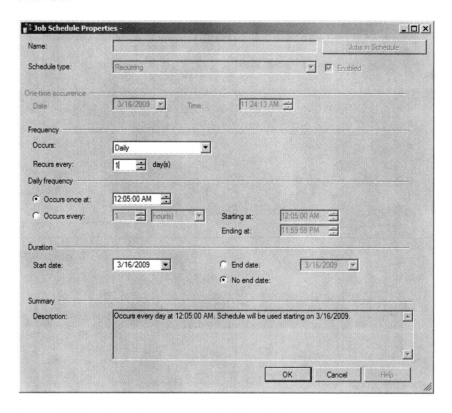

Figure 5|22 > Snapshot Agent Job Schedule Properties

You'll be returned to the **Snapshot Agent** screen, as shown in Figure 5|23. This time you should notice that the text box says the Agent will run every day, instead of every 14 days. Check both of the check boxes to have the Snapshot created immediately and to have the **Snapshot Agent** run every day, then click **Next**.

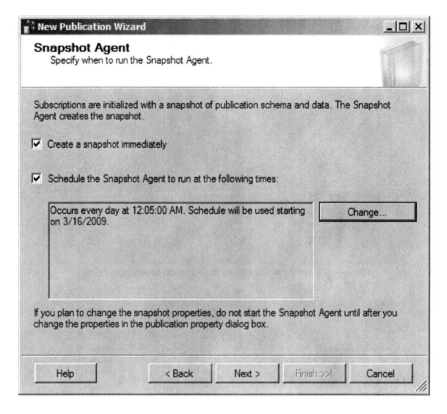

Figure 5|23 > Snapshot Agent

The **Agent Security** screen, shown in Figure 5|24, is where you set up the account under which the **Snapshot Agent** process will run. Click **Security Settings**.

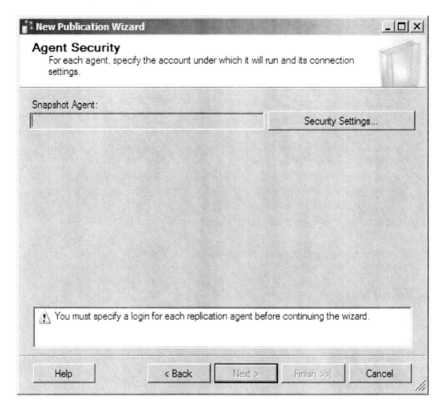

Figure 5|24 > Agent Security

In the **Snapshot Agent Security** dialog box, shown in Figure 5|25, select the **Run under the following Windows account** radio button and enter **SYNCDOMAIN\syncuser** in the **Process account** text box. Next, type **P@ssw0rd** in the **Password** and **Confirm Password** text boxes. In the **Connect to the Publisher** section, ensure the **By impersonating the process account** radio button is selected. Running this process under the Domain user account you created at the beginning of the book, and utilizing impersonation, ensures that you're following security best practices. Click **OK**.

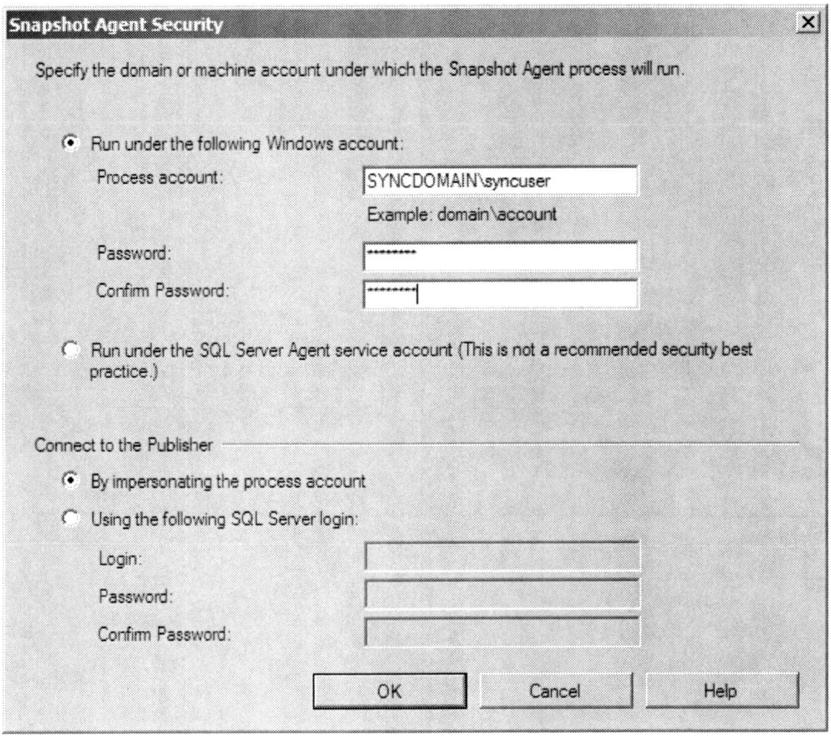

Figure 5|25 > Snapshot Agent Security

The **Agent Security** screen, shown in Figure 5|26, should now reflect the addition of the **SYNCDOMAIN\syncuser** user account in the **Snapshot Agent** text box. Click **Next**.

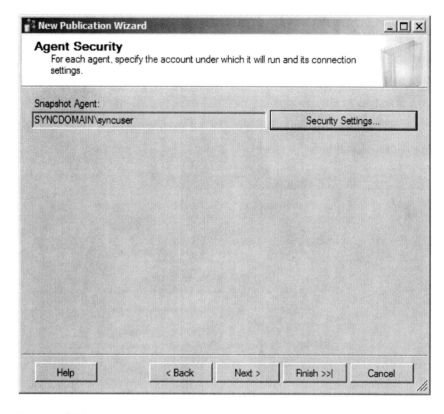

Figure 5|26 > Agent Security

The **Wizard Actions** screen, shown in Figure 5|27, lets you specify what actions occur when you reach the end of the **New Publication Wizard**. You definitely want to create the publication, and a script would be helpful to recreate all these steps you just took, so check both check boxes and then click **Next**.

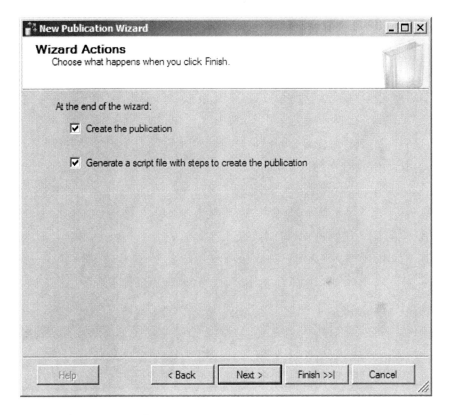

Figure 5|27 > Wizard Actions

The **Script File Properties** screen, shown in Figure 5|28, lets you specify the location where the script file will be created at the end of the **New Publication Wizard.** Select **Overwrite the existing file**, act globally by using **International text,** and then click **Next**.

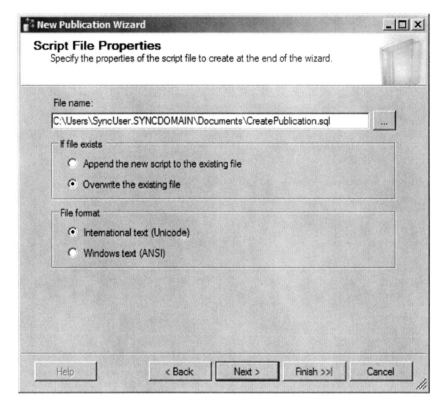

Figure 5|28 > Script File Properties

In the **Complete the Wizard** screen, shown in Figure 5|29, enter **ContosoBottlingPub** in the **Publication name** text box. Review the actions listed to be executed and click **Finish** if they're correct.

Figure 5|29 > Complete the Wizard

The **Creating Publication** screen, shown in Figure 3|30, will display the progress of configuring the Distributor, creating the Publication, adding the articles, adding the join filters, starting the Snapshot Agent, and generating the script file. If everything is successful, click **Close**.

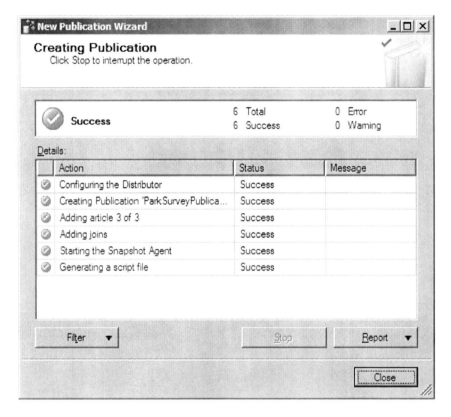

Figure 5|30 > Creating Publication

Guess what? You're done.

Summary

In this chapter, I walked you through the creation of a Publication, based on the ContosoBottling database. Hopefully, you now grasp the power of things such as conflict resolvers, row filters and join filters to make your system work exactly the way you want it to. The fact that SQL Server Merge Replication is the most powerful and sophisticated data synchronization technology in the world sometimes presents a double-edged sword to developers and database administrators.

The ability to create your own conflict resolvers with stored procedures and .NET is a powerful capability, with the potential to solve synchronization conflicts in a way that's not possible by the built-in resolvers. That being said, a poorly-written resolver, or one that includes an extreme amount of business logic, can slow SQL Server down or create unintended issues that negate its usefulness. Keep your custom resolvers as simple as they can be, while still solving your business problem, and you'll be in great shape.

Reducing the amount of data sent out to Subscribers via the Static and Parameterized filtering of rows, and the ability to join those filters to other tables, is a powerful tool to ensure that the right people get the right data. Keep in mind that SQL Server executes the filter logic you create line-by-line every time a Subscriber synchronizes. As you might imagine, including too many filters, or creating filter hierarchies more than four levels deep, has the potential to strip SQL Server of its performance.

Imagine that SQL Server without any filters is a fast V8 engine.

Adding Static filters with fixed values and simple Parameterized filters can result in a performance hit of up to 15%, taking your V8 down to a V6.

Adding complex Parameterized filters with deep hierarchies to the mix has the potential to reduce your performance by up to 50%, taking your V8 down to an inline 4, if misused or overused.

SQL Server gives you all the rope you need to hang yourself when it comes to filtering, and I've seen organizations that have done just that, wondering why their performance and scalability is so bad. Like so many things in life, moderation is the key; use only the absolute minimum amount of filter logic needed to accomplish your goals. If you need more business logic, I would err on the side of sending too much data to the Subscriber and execute needed logic there.

I don't want to scare you away from using these great technologies; I just want you to use them wisely so that you and your users will be delighted with the system you've constructed. In the next chapter, I'll take you on a deep dive of all the things you need to do to make your Publisher as fast and scalable as possible.

Chapter 6 > Configuring the Publisher

Chapter Takeaways

The purpose of this chapter is to build upon what you've created with the Publication Wizard. The Publisher is the heart of the system and I think it's important to take you under the hood to show you how everything works. Some of the things I'm going to tell you might seem arcane if you're just building a workgroup solution. For those of you who are using this technology in order to mobilize your entire organization, this knowledge will be critical to your success in the performance and scalability departments.

Publication Properties

From the **Object Explorer**, expand the **Replication** and **Local Publications** folders, right-click on **ContosoBottling** and select **Properties,** as shown in Figure 6|1.

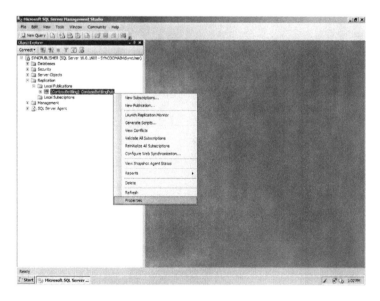

Figure 6|1 > Local Publications Properties

The **Publication Properties** dialog box, shown in Figure 6|2, appears and contains every choice you made during your journey through the **New Publication Wizard**. If you need to revise any choices, this is the place to do it. I will walk you through several different Property Pages, not only to accomplish tasks that can only be performed here, but also to do things that you could have done back in the wizard. Let's start out with the **General** Page, since you're already looking at it.

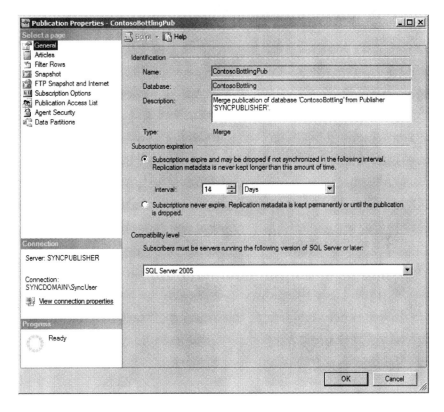

Figure 6|2 > Publication Properties

The key area I want you to focus on is the **Subscription expiration** section. As you can see, the default setting results in a subscription being dropped if a Subscriber doesn't synchronize within a 14-day period. Actually, it's 15 days because SQL Server adds another day to account for world time zones, just in case. If you don't sync SSCE within this interval, you have to start over via re-initialization. Also, if you ever find yourself using a Republisher, make sure its Subscription expiration interval is shorter than that of the Publisher to which it's subscribing.

Subscription expiration is a big deal because SQL Server utilizes quite a few metadata tables to track changes for Merge Replication. As these tables go about their business of tracking changes for users who haven't synched in a while, they can grow to a point where they start to slow down the whole system, due to excessive locking and blocking, and the only thing that reins them in is the Subscription expiration interval. When a Subscription expires because a user hasn't synched for an amount of time that exceeds the Subscription interval you defined, all the metadata being tracked for that particular Subscriber is deleted from the system, reducing the load on the system. Therefore, you should try to make the Subscription expiration interval as small as possible in order to minimize the amount of tracked data. If you know that your users have to sync every workday, then set the interval to 3 days to account for normal and 3-day weekends.

I can't mention these metadata tables without telling you what's going on under the hood. The **MSmerge_contents** table is used to track INSERTs and UPDATEs and the **MSmerge_tombstone** table is used to track the DELETEs. To facilitate change tracking, SQL Server adds 3 triggers to each table defined as an Article in a Publication. Remember the Uniqueidentifier column that SQL

Server adds to each of your tables during the Publication Wizard? The GUIDs found in each of row of these columns is how SQL Server tracks each row. When a table's trigger fires, due to a DML operation, the GUIDs of the affected rows are inserted into the **MSmerge_contents** and **MSmerge_tombstone** tables. As you might imagine, the **MSmerge_contents** table can get very large and this can be a cause for concern. SQL Server also inserts a row in another table called **MSmerge_genhistory** to group these operations together in something called a generation.

A generation is just an integer that's used to track this logical group of INSERTs, UPDATEs and DELETEs for a particular Article table. A generation's status is marked as open while this grouping of DML operations is taking place for a given Article. When an unfiltered sync begins, the Merge Agent calls **sp_MSmakegeneration** to set the generation status to closed in order to prevent any new changes from being added into an existing generation, and then a new generation is opened. Meanwhile, the Merge Agent calls **sp_MSenumchanges,** which joins **MSmerge_genhistory** to **MSmerge_contents** and **MSmerge_tombstone** in order to figure out which rows need to be synched with a given Subscriber. Groups of generations are batched together and the sync process begins.

If your Publication uses parameterized filters, the **MSmerge_partition_groups** table is used and contains a row for each data subset as a result of differing HOST_NAME values being sent from synchronizing Subscribers. The **MSmerge_current_ partition_mappings** table holds one row for each row in **MSmerge_contents** belonging to a particular partition. If you were worried about a large **MSmerge_contents** table, try multiplying that by all the different partitions you might have and

you've got the **MSmerge_current_partition_mappings** table.
Another table called **MSmerge_past_partition_mappings** gets a
row inserted for each partition that also has a deleted a row in
MSmerge_tombstone. It can also get a row if the value of filtered
column changes, resulting in data that moves out of the partition.
The **MSmerge_generation_partition_mappings** table tracks
whether a particular generation contains changes relevant to a
given partition, and can become massive in size. During a filtered
sync, **sp_MSmakegeneration** has added importance for filtered
tables because it has to populate the
MSmerge_generation_partition _mappings table with data for
changes relevant to a given partition, which can be a lot of work. I
recommend you manually or automatically call this stored
procedure whenever a big DML operation is performed directly
against SQL Server. A potentially slow 5-way join is executed by
sp_MSenumchanges. where
MSmerge_generation_partition_mappings is joined to
MSmerge_current_partition_mappings, **MSmerge_contents**,
MSmerge_past_partition_mappings and **MSmerge_tombstone**
to figure out which changes are relevant to a Subscriber's
partition. You can avoid a lot of this pain if none of your partitions
are overlapping and you define your filters as such, by specifying
that a row from a filtered table will only go to one Subscription.

I'm going to apologize now for making you endure the particulars
of all these Merge Replication system tables that make everything
work. Besides knowing how the system ticks, the big takeaway is
that these tables will do more to slow down your Publisher than
any other factor. These tables will be the source of more activity
than the tables you're actually publishing. They will rapidly
change in size, which can lead to outdated statistics and
fragmented indexes, resulting in slower performance. You

definitely want to avoid all the extra locking, blocking, deadlocking, and timeouts that can arise from this situation. Therefore, you need to combat these potential issues proactively by rebuilding or defragmenting their indexes, updating statistics, and spreading database files across multiple spindles. I'll show you how to do this at the end of the chapter, when I discuss ongoing maintenance activities.

The **Compatibility level** section at the bottom dictates which version of SQL Server the Subscribers must be running. This is mainly about data types since SQL Server 2008 supports new ones, like geospatial, that aren't supported by SQL Server 2005. You might find it odd that I have SQL Server 2005 selected on the screen. I have this for two reasons:

1. Support for SQL Server Mobile 3.0 or SQL Server Compact 3.1 that's found in ROM on Windows Mobile 6.x devices.
2. Support for Republishing where the final Subscriber might be SQL Server Compact. This is interesting because even if the Publisher and Republisher are both running SQL Server 2008, a final Subscriber of SQL Server Compact will cause the Publication on the Republisher to fail, due to data type mismatches.

Additionally, any Publisher or Republisher that has SQL Server Compact Subscribers communicating directly with them must create Snapshot files that are in character format.

Selecting **Articles** from the **Select a page** section will display a tree view of all the tables and columns available to publish, as shown in Figure 6|3. Here, you get the opportunity to make changes to choices you made previously during the Publication Wizard. These changes could include things such as download-only tables, row or column-level tracking, or what kind of conflict resolver you want to use.

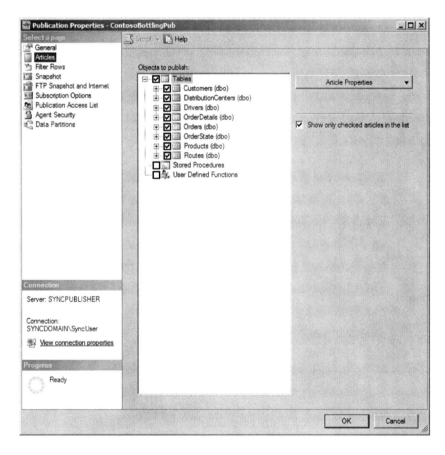

Figure 6|3 > Articles

Selecting **Filter Rows** from the **Select a page** section will display a
tree view of all the filters and Join filters, as shown in Figure 6|4.
If you need to add, edit, or delete any static or parameterized
filters, this is place to do it. Use this property page as a place to
perform deep analysis of your filters and their effect on the
performance of your system. Keep your filter depths to 4 or less
and use them to tell you which columns to index in affected
tables. This is also the best place to verify that your filter queries
are simple and don't contain IN clauses, sub-selects, or any kind of
circular logic that can torpedo your performance and scalability.

Figure 6|4 > Filter Rows

On your root-level HOST_NAME filters, use non-overlapping
partitions if possible, by specifying that you'll send filtered table
rows to only one Subscription. Additionally, ensure that you
specify **Unique Key** joins for all your joined table filters.
Remember that filtering is performed on a row-by-row basis,
which has a profound impact on the throughput of your data.

Selecting **Snapshot** from the **Select a page** section will display the page shown in Figure 6|5. Here, you can change your Snapshot format from native to character depending on your Subscriber type. You can also point to a different UNC server and share, as needed, if elements of your system architecture changes. Keep in mind, you can increase your system fault-tolerance even farther by using Microsoft's Distributed File System (DFS) for your Snapshot share.

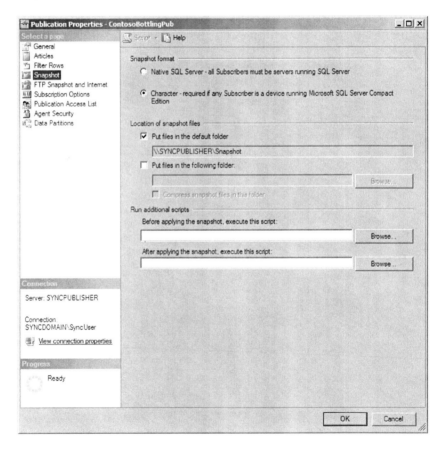

Figure 6|5 > Snapshot

Selecting **FTP Snapshot and Internet** from the **Select a page** section will display the page shown in Figure 6|6. As you can see on the screen, the check box at the top is unchecked, since we don't use FTP to copy our Snapshots. The check box at the bottom is checked because our SQL Server Compact Subscribers will all be synchronizing through IIS.

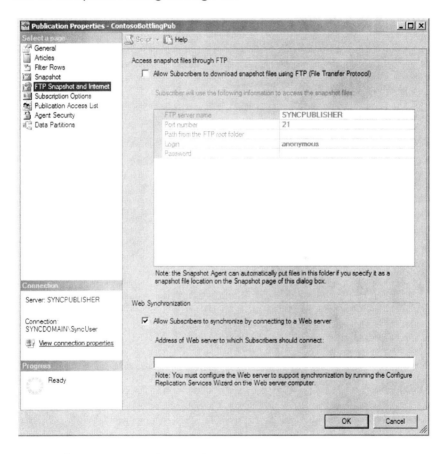

Figure 6|6 > FTP Snapshot and Internet

Selecting **Subscription Options** from the **Select a page** section will display a page that is critical to the performance of your Publication, as shown in Figure 6|7. I'm not concerned with the **Conflict Reporting** and **Creation and Synchronization** sections, so leave those values alone. If you've created any filters for your Publication, then **Allow parameterized filters** in the Filtering section should be set to True.

Figure 6|7 > Subscription Options

The **Validate Subscribers** setting should have a value of HOST_NAME() if you're using parameterized filters to create subsets of data for different Subscribers.

In order to give your system the best performance possible, **Precompute partitions** should be set to True. This option tells SQL Server to figure out in advance which data rows belong to a particular Subscriber's partition. It performs a partition evaluation based on a Subscriber's filters and persists the results of the evaluation so that when a Subscriber synchronizes with the Publisher, it can start downloading those changes right away, instead of waiting for an evaluation to happen on the fly. This results in a dramatic performance improvement for all your synchronizing Subscribers. This option can only be used if your filters meet criteria related to the use of dynamic and nondeterministic functions, as well as circular join filter relationships. You can determine if your filters are valid by running the **sp_check_subset_filter** stored procedure. Due to the extra work required to precompute the subsets of data, DML operations performed directly against SQL Server may sometimes take longer than expected, depending on the complexity of your schema and filters. Consider enabling the READ_COMMITTED_SNAPSHOT database option before creating the Publication to use row versioning instead of locking to reduce contention between database users and replication activity.

ALTER DATABASE ContosoBottling
    SET READ_COMMITTED_SNAPSHOT ON;

Break **tempdb** into many files and spread it out across numerous dedicated spindles because it's going to get a workout. Also, make sure it has plenty of room because it will stop versioning rows if it runs out of space.

Optimize synchronization should be set to False, since its functionality has been superseded by precomputed partitions. It should only be used if your filters don't meet the criteria required by precomputed partitions. This optimization prevents all other Subscriptions from being affected by a partition change made by a particular Subscriber. Use this feature in conjunction with setting the value of the Snapshot Agent profile parameter **MaxNetworkOptimization** equal to 1.

In the **Merge Processes** section, I want you to set **Limit concurrent processes** to True. A setting of False would allow an unlimited number of Merge Agents to run simultaneously, which could bring SQL Server to its knees with excessive locking, blocking, and deadlocking.

For the **Maximum concurrent processes** setting, I want you to set that value equal to half the number of processor cores found in your server. Keep in mind that I'm talking cores, not processors. If you have a 16-core server, then I want you to set it to 8. I know, it sounds like you're wasting the other 8 cores instead of utilizing them to get more work done. Keep in mind that Merge Agent utilizes more than one thread to perform work and I really don't like to allocate more than one thread to each core if I can help it. Consider the setting of half the number of cores in your server to be a starting point. After you've configured your entire Merge Replication infrastructure, test it under an actual Subscriber load, or via a test harness, and determine for yourself if you can increase the number of concurrent processes. Always raise it by a factor of 2 each time you feel certain that you can bump it up. Remember that you'll need to add an additional IIS server for every 2 additional concurrent processes you want to support.

In the last section, I want you to set **Replicate schema changes** to True. I don't know anyone who gets their schema right the first time around, so it's important to be able to make schema changes and push them down to Subscribers as needed.

To ensure that all your intended Subscribers can sync, go to the **Select a page** section and click **Publication Access List**, as shown in Figure 6|8. You'll notice that SyncUser is already added to the list of approved Subscribers, due to the fact that you made this user the SQL Server Administrator back in Chapter 4 about the Distributor. To ensure that other desired users and groups can sync, go to the **Security | Logins** folders in the **Object Explorer** and make sure that the appropriate Logins have been created. Additionally, map those Logins to the ContosoBottling database.

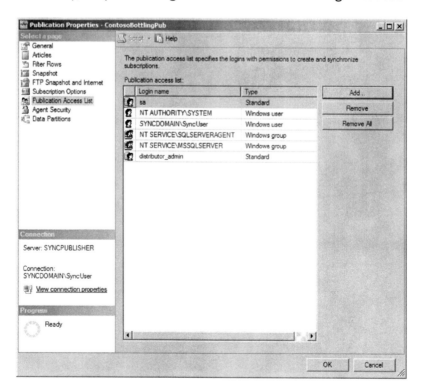

Figure 6|8 > Publication Access List

Click **Add** to bring up the **Add Publication Access** dialog box, as shown in Figure 6|9. Note that the only way your designated Domain user or group will show up in this dialog is if you've already defined the account at the **Publisher**. Select the Domain user or group account you just added as a SQL Login and click **OK** to give them rights to sync.

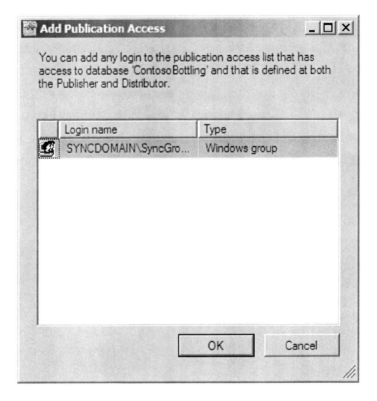

Figure 6|9 > Add Publication Access

Selecting **Agent Security** from the **Select a page** section will display a page that shows which Domain user account is being used to run the Snapshot Agent, as shown in Figure 6|10. Not much to do here, unless you want to change the Domain user account.

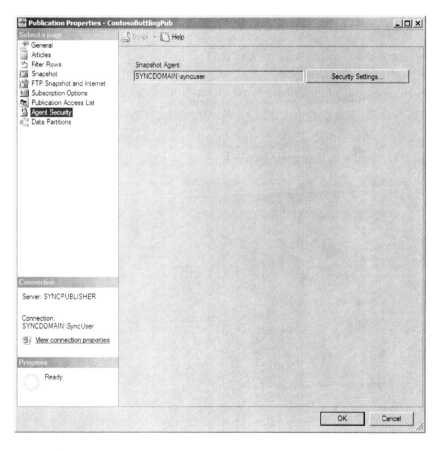

Figure 6|10 > Agent Security

Select **Data Partitions** from the **Select a page** section to display a page that allows you to define data partitions for Publications that utilize parameterized filters, as shown in Figure 6|11. It's crucial that you take advantage of the features found on this screen to ensure that filtered database initializations and re-initializations from SQL Server Compact don't leave your users waiting.

The first thing I want you to do is to check the check box at the bottom of the screen, which allows for the automatic generation of filtered data Snapshots without manual intervention from your DBA whenever a new Subscriber attempts to synchronize. The ability to pre-generate filtered data Snapshots and refresh them on a schedule is the main reason for this page, and it's all about performance. To get started, click **Add**.

Figure 6|11 > Data Partitions

In the **Add Data Partition** dialog, shown in Figure 6|12, enter the filter value sent by a Subscriber during a synchronization in the **HOST_NAME** text box. Since I want these filtered Snapshots to contain the freshest data possible, allowing their creation to happen on demand isn't good enough, so check the **Schedule the Snapshot Agent for this partition to run at the following time(s)** checkbox and click **Change**.

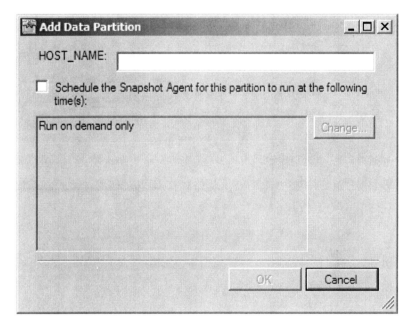

Figure 6|12 > Add Data Partition

The familiar **Job Schedule Properties** dialog will appear, as shown in Figure 6|13. If you remember the Publication Wizard in Chapter 5, I had you use this same dialog to create a new schema Snapshot every night. I want you to do the same thing with filtered Snapshots so that fresh data is provided to Subscribers on a nightly basis.

You'll first need to determine how long it takes to create a filtered Snapshot and then stagger Snapshot creation time appropriately. Next, plan on concurrently creating Snapshots that match half the number of processor cores on your SQL Server. Finally, ensure that you have a maintenance window available when the servers are not being utilized by Subscribers, in order to kick off these jobs. I'm hoping that will be every night, but if you have tens of thousands of Subscribers, you may need to break that up across evenings and weekends. Therefore, keep the frequency to **Daily,** with a **1**-day recurrence if possible, and click **OK**.

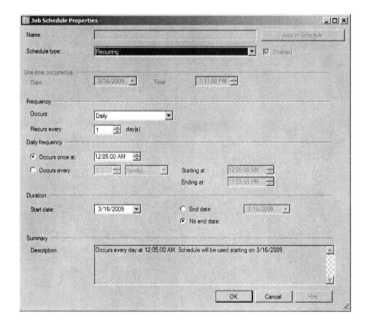

Figure 6|13 > Job Schedule Properties

The **Add Data Partition** dialog, shown in Figure 6|14, now reflects my last name or some jewelry store as the **HOST_NAME** filter value. It also shows that a filtered Snapshot will be refreshed every night at 12:05 AM. Click **OK**.

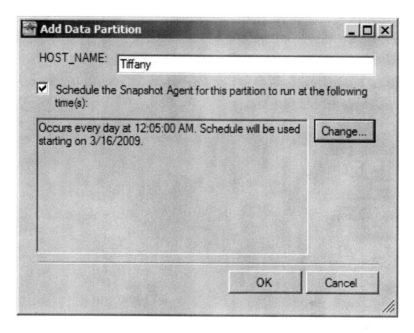

Figure 6|14 > Add Data Partition

The **Data Partition** page, shown in Figure 6|15, now displays an entry for the creation of a Snapshot at the top of the list view. You can highlight the row and click **Edit** to make changes to the schedule or click **Delete** to remove this job. Highlighting one or more rows and clicking **Generate the selected snapshots now** will immediately create Snapshots based on their respective filtered partitions. Doing the same thing, but clicking **Clean up the existing snapshots,** will clean up metadata. Click **OK** to close the **Publication Properties** dialog.

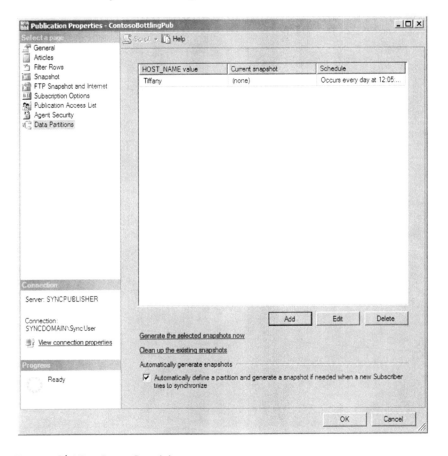

Figure 6|15 > Data Partitions

If a schema Snapshot hasn't been created yet, I want you to right-click on your **ContosoBottling** Publication as you've done before, and select **View Snapshot Agent Status**. This will bring up a dialog called **View Snapshot Agent Status – ContosoBottlingPub**. From here, you can start and stop Snapshots and monitor the health of your **Publication**. I want you to click the **Start** button to create a Snapshot, as shown in Figure 6|16. The **Status** text box will let you know when the process is complete for your articles. If the Snapshot creation fails, double-check to make sure that **SyncUser** is an Administrator on SYNCPUBLISHER.

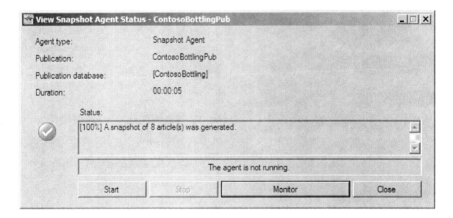

Figure 6|16 > View Snapshot Agent Status

Since you already have the **View Snapshot Agent Status –
ContosoBottlingPub** dialog open, I want you to click the **Monitor**
button in order to launch the **Replication Monitor**, as shown in
Figure 6|17.

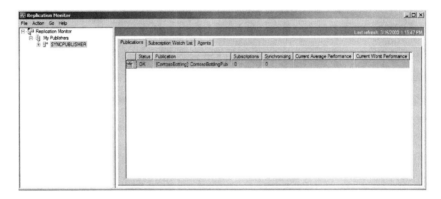

Figure 6|17 > Replication Monitor

This tool is a hidden gem that provides real-time information
about the Contoso Bottling Publication and all your Subscriptions.
From the default Publications tab, you can see the total number
of Subscribers that have subscribed to your Publication, the
number of Subscribers that are currently synchronizing, and the
average and worst performance metrics. Selecting the
Subscription Watch List tab will display individual information
about all of the Subscribers, including things such as performance,
data delivery rate, and sync durations. Moving over to the
Common Jobs tab reveals the current status of various SQL Server
Jobs that have been pre-built in order to aid in maintenance of
the Publisher and Distributor.

This kind of instrumentation is worth its weight in gold when it
comes to monitoring, tuning, and troubleshooting your system.

Performance Tuning

I've shared most of my SQL Server Publisher performance and scalability best practices with you in the various sections of this chapter. That said, there are still a number of recommendations without a home, due to their non-relevance to one of those sections or otherwise. Therefore, I am going to list them off for you here in rapid-fire succession. Welcome to the lightning-round of performance tuning:

- Ensure that your Windows Server has one CPU core and 2 GB or RAM for every 100 concurrent Subscribers you want to support. That being said, I always want you to start out conservatively when it comes to creating a load on your servers. Having a 16-core server with 32 GB of RAM doesn't mean you can support 1,600 concurrent Subscribers right out of the gate. I want you to start at half that number and work your way up based on real-world load-testing.
- Turn off Hyperthreading because it's been shown to decrease SQL Server's I/O performance, rather than enhance it. SQL Server's scheduler can grab a Hyperthread thinking it's a real processor core and ends up sadly disappointed by the lack of horsepower.
- De-normalize your database schema, or use a mapping table, to reduce number of tables in joins to boost performance. This is relevant on SQL Server with its join filters, as well as on SQL Server Compact when your .NET application needs to perform multi-table joins.
- Don't add your own user-defined triggers to execute business logic against a Published database, as they will slow down the synchronization of changes.

- Index the columns used in static and parameterized row and join filtering. This will reduce the workload on your CPU cores and memory, while yielding significantly faster performance. Using less CPU horsepower and allocating less memory because SQL Server isn't performing table scans means better scalability, because there will be spare CPU cycles and memory registers for other Subscribers.
- Add one or more Filegroup(s) to your database to contain multiple, secondary database files spread out across many physical disks. This will increase your I/O performance, since SQL Server can use multiple threads to perform operations that span multiple disks in parallel. This boost will be especially apparent when tables used in join filter queries are on different physical disks. Additionally, placing those heavily utilized Merge Replication system tables in different files across dedicated disks will make a dramatic performance and scalability difference for your system.
- Limit use of large object types such as text, ntext, image, varchar(max), nvarchar(max) or varbinary(max), as they require a significant memory allocation and will negatively impact performance. If you must use them to send a byte array from a captured signature or something similar, put those columns in a separate table with a one-to-one relationship with the row data to which they belong.
- Use SQL Server 2008 and Windows Server 2008 together because together, they take better advantage of the next-generation networking stack, dramatically increasing network throughput.

- Increase a Host Bus Adapter's (HBA) queue depth to 64 in order for SQL Server to see substantial gains in I/O performance.
- Set the minimum and maximum memory usage to within 4 GB of total system memory, utilizing SQL Server's ability to set a minimum and maximum amount of memory that it will use. This will boost SQL Server's responsiveness, since it won't have to dynamically allocate memory on the fly to respond to increased loads. It will also reduce memory fragmentation, since SQL Server will get all the memory it needs and never have to relinquish it back to Windows Server.
- Set Max Degree of Parallelism = 1 in order to suppress the generation of parallel query plans. Merge Replication already has too many concurrent processes performing work without introducing another one that might increase the level of locking and blocking.
- Tempdb gets hammered more than any other database in SQL Server. It's used for temporary tables, storing intermediate results, sorting, row versioning, and many other tasks. It can grow wildly when autogrowth is enabled. This means that whenever tempdb has to grow, it freezes SQL Server to do so which has a negative impact on performance. The best plan of attack to deal with tempdb is to break it up into multiple files equal to the number of processor cores to increase disk bandwidth. Next, ensure those files are spread across multiple dedicated disks so that other database files aren't impacted by disk I/O contention. Then, pre-allocate space for all the tempdb files by setting their file sizes to a value large enough to handle the most demanding workloads without expanding. Finally, set the auto-growth increment

to 10% so it's less likely to have to expand frequently. Each file must be the same size, with the same auto-growth setting.

- Database data files should reside on separate disks from transaction logs. As mentioned in the previous bullet, the tempdb files should be on their own disks and I want you to place the Snapshot share on its own disks as well. In the proper terminology of Storage Area Networks (SAN), I want all these database objects on their own unshared, dedicated LUNs, as shown in Figure 6|18. No matter what your SAN vendor tells you, building a single aggregate LUN across all your disks is not acceptable. When it comes to database performance, virtualized LUN volumes that don't represent dedicated spindles are also unacceptable.

OS + SQL
RAID 5 Internal (3 Disks)
Windows Server 2008,
SQL Server 2008

Tempdb.mdf
Pre-sized w/
10% auto-growth
Tempdb
Dedicated RAID
10 LUN (6 Disks)

Data
Dedicated RAID
10 LUN (6 Disks)
Master.mdf,
Model.mdf,
MSDBData.mdf,
Distribution.mdf,
Publication.mdf

Snapshot File Share
Snapshot
Dedicated RAID
10 LUN (6 Disks)

Logs
Dedicated RAID
10 LUN (6 Disks)
Mastlog.ldf,
Modellog.ldf,
MSDBLog.ldf,
Templog.ldf,
Distribution.ldf,
Publication_log.ldf

Figure 6|18 > Unshared LUNs

Just as with Tempdb, break up your database into multiple files, equal to half of your processor cores, to increase disk bandwidth. Each file must be the same size with the same auto-growth setting. This allows SQL to stripe allocations across files in a round-robin fashion, which spreads I/O across several LUNs.

While we're talking disks, I have some pretty clear-cut rules:

Faster is always better. More is better. Sharing is bad.

This means high-speed disks, a fast data bus, and the fastest form of RAID. Take a look at the tables below and see if you can guess which combination I would always recommend:

Disks

Disk Speed	Latency
4,200 RPM	7.2 ms
5,400 RPM	5.6 ms
7,200 RPM	4.2 ms
10,000 RPM	3 ms
15,000 RPM	2 ms

Data Bus

Bus Type	Speed
Serial ATA (SATA)	300 Mbps
SCSI	320 Mbps
Serial Attached SCSI (SAS)	375 Mbps
iSCSI	125 Mbps
Fibre Channel	425 Mbps

RAID

RAID Type	Comments
0 (Striping)	Fast but no redundancy
1 (Mirroring)	Redundancy but single-disk writes
5 (Striping + Parity)	Redundancy but slow writes
10 (Striping + Mirroring)	Redundancy and fast writes

You guessed it right! I'll always recommend RAID 10 over RAID 5 because of significantly faster writes and fewer operations per write. Fibre Channel reigns supreme but if you can't afford it, go with SAS. Last but not least, 15,000 RPM drives are the only way to go. When you're building a SAN, use as many disk spindles as possible in order to create lots of dedicated LUNs, so you can spread out your data and log files for best performance.

Ongoing Maintenance

Now that you've finished building this high performance sport car, you've got to maintain it. You didn't think this thing would run on auto-pilot did you?

Indexes and Statistics

Well, it can run on auto-pilot, but as users repeatedly synchronize data over time, the database grows and changes in ways that can degrade performance. Luckily, this kind of degradation is preventable.

I've mentioned previously in this chapter that those Merge Replication system tables with really long names will be responsible for more activity than any of table on SQL Server. The constant stream of DML operations against these tables means that they can lose their density as indexes become fragmented. Large data changes can occur that don't necessarily meet the threshold of the auto-update statistics, causing them to become outdated, and SQL Server is left with bad query plans that yield poor performance. The system tables you need to optimize can be found in the Object Explorer by expanding Databases | ContosoBottling | Tables | System Tables:

- MSmerge_contents
- MSmerge_tombstone
- MSmerge_genhistory
- MSmerge_current_partition_mappings
- MSmerge_past_partition_mappings
- MSmerge_generation_partition_mappings

You can manually rebuild the indexes on the tables above by expanding the table, right-clicking on **Indexes,** selecting Rebuild All, and clicking OK at the bottom of the Rebuild Indexes dialog. I recommend you perform this task at least once per day during a nightly maintenance window. Building an SQL Server Job that automatically rebuilds the appropriate indexes for you by calling ALTER INDEX will keep you from doing this manually on your production servers. You should also rebuild the indexes on all of the user tables of the database you've published on a weekly basis.

As far as statistics go, if your latest DML operation just pumped 20,000,000 new records into the **MSmerge_generation_partition _mappings** table, your query execution plan might not be optimal anymore. While SQL Server is configured to updates statistics for you automatically, it doesn't mean that it can't fall behind if it's too busy. An example of extreme stress that might make SQL Server too busy is if you have an ETL operation coming from DB2 on a Mainframe every minute that's rapidly changing the number of rows in your Publication's tables while still servicing thousands of Subscribers. This suboptimal situation can be further compounded by complex and unwieldy filters. In a case like this, SQL Server might need a little help from you. As your first line of defense, create a SQL Server Job that runs the following stored procedure, shown below, during your nightly maintenance window:

```
use <Database Name>
go
exec sp_updatestats
go
```

Additionally, you can execute a more powerful and targeted SQL Server command against the Merge Replication system tables that will keep statistics up-to-date after big DML operations by calling:

```
UPDATE STATISTICS <table name> WITH FULLSCAN
```

Depending on the frequency of the large DML operations, you can run this job as often as you need to. In the end, this will give the optimizer a better query plan and force stored procedures to recompile. Another good time to run this job is after you run the jobs to rebuild the indexes of all your Merge Replication system tables. While this may be new territory for some of you, I want to ensure all bases are covered.

Backup and Restore

Another kind of ongoing maintenance that everyone's accustomed to performing is database backups and restores to maximize your data availability. Since there are already plenty of resources on full and differential backups, I won't be taking you on a deep dive here. For Merge Replication, I want you to backup the Publication, Distribution, MSDB, and Master databases during your maintenance window. Additionally, ensure that you restore your backups to the same server where they were created to preserve the replication settings.

Publication and Schema Changes

At some point along the way, you might want to alter which tables and columns are replicated down to the Subscriber. You can always do this by bringing up the **Publication Properties** dialog, selecting **Articles**, and changing the check box selections you've made. You will then have to create a new schema Snapshot and filtered Snapshots for all your partitions, and each device must reinitialize their Subscription.

If you're looking to change any aspect of the Publication database schema, you must make those changes via T-SQL statements, not through the graphical tools provided to you by the SQL Server Management Studio. This is because Management Studio attempts to drop and recreate tables, which doesn't work with Published objects. Therefore, any changes you wish to make and propagate to the SQL Server Compact Subscribers must be accomplished through variations on the ALTER TABLE DDL statement. This lets you add, drop, or modify columns and some - but not all - constraints. Remember to make schema changes only on the Publisher and not on a Republisher or Subscriber. Schema changes made to the Publisher will flow through any Republishers and on to the Subscribers. Oftentimes, this will require the creation of a new Snapshot and each device must reinitialize their Subscription.

Performance Analysis

The last element of ongoing maintenance with which I want you to concern yourself is the use of the Performance Monitor. This tool should be used to keep track of various performance metrics, so you know when things are working well and when you have a problem on your hands. The most relevant system objects and performance counters are as follows:

- **Processor Object: % Processor Time:** This counter represents the percentage of processor utilization. A value over 80% is a CPU bottleneck.
- **System Object: Processor Queue Length:** This counter represents the number of threads that are delayed in the processor Ready Queue and waiting to be scheduled for execution. A value over 2 is bottleneck and shows that there is more work available than the processor can handle. Remember to divide the value by the number of processor cores on your server.
- **Memory Object: Available Mbytes:** This counter represents the amount of physical memory available for allocation to a process, or for system use. Values below 10% of total system RAM indicate that you need to add additional RAM to your server.
- **PhysicalDisk Object: % Disk Time:** This counter represents the percentage of time that the selected disk is busy responding to read or write requests. A value greater than 50% is an I/O bottleneck.
- **PhysicalDisk Object: Average Disk Queue Length:** This counter represents the average number of read/write requests that are queued on a given physical disk. If your disk queue length is greater than 2, you've got an I/O

bottleneck with too many read/write operations waiting to be performed.

- **PhysicalDisk Object: Average Disk Seconds/Read and Disk Seconds/Write:** These counters represent the average time in seconds of a read or write of data to and from a disk. A value of less than 10 ms is what you're shooting for in terms of best performance. You can get by with subpar values between 10 – 20 ms, but anything above that is considered slow. Times above 50 ms represent a very serious I/O bottleneck.

- **PhysicalDisk Object: Average Disk Reads/Second and Disk Writes/Second:** These counters represent the rate of read and write operations against a given disk. You need to ensure that these values stay below 85% of a disk's capacity, by adding disks or reducing the load from SQL Server. Disk access times will increase exponentially when you get beyond 85% capacity.

Keep in mind with the above disk counters that in RAID 0, 5 and 10, you will need to divide the performance counter values by the number of disks. In RAID 1, you'll need to divide the values by 2.

Your Service Level Agreement (SLA) to your Subscribers is keeping your system within the acceptable performance parameters listed above.

Summary

In this chapter, I've taken you on a tour of all the Publication properties. It would be an understatement to say that some of these properties required a deep dive to help you understand what's going on. As you can see, no one individual element of the Publication is powerful enough to make the whole system perform well. All elements must be tuned and follow performance and scalability best practices.

The most important thing you have to get right is the database schema with its filters. It must be carefully designed with the right data types, Primary and Foreign Key relationships, and indexes, and not too much normalization. The tables should never have too many columns, and the filters should never cause the system to return too many rows. Remember that the goal of filtering is not to create business logic, but to direct subsets of data to different Subscribers. The goal should never be to send you entire corporate database to SQL Server Compact. Send just enough data to the Subscribers so they can do their job - and nothing more.

Keep it simple out there.

Chapter 7 > Server Agent

Chapter Takeaways

IIS serves as the Internet gateway that links laptops, Netbooks and Windows Mobile devices running SQL Server Compact to SQL Server in your data center. It's here that SQL Server's binary Merge Replication protocol is converted into a format that runs over HTTP(S) and can therefore traverse routers and firewalls. The purpose of this chapter is to walk you through the installation of various IIS and SQL Server components, as well as the SSCE Server Tools on the IIS tier of this architecture. With the prerequisites installed, you'll navigate through the Web Synchronization wizard to install, register, and configure the SSCE Server Agent in order to facilitate communications with SSCE Subscribers. I'll then show you how to optimize your installation for performance, as well as troubleshoot it with a variety of diagnostic tools.

Domain Considerations

The Server Agent tier of the replication environment resides inside the corporate network behind the firewall, and this IIS server must be joined to SYNCDOMAIN. Additionally, the SYNCDOMAIN\Syncuser domain user account should be added to the local Administrators group on the IIS server. Once this is complete, logoff the IIS server and re-logon as SYNCDOMAIN\syncuser. Do this with all your load-balanced IIS servers. If your company uses a DMZ network security configuration, place your IIS servers behind the back firewall.

IIS 6.0 Management Compatibility Components

In order to get the SSCE Server Tools to work properly on Windows Server 2008 and IIS 7, you need to install the IIS 6.0 Management Compatibility Components, via the Windows Server 2008 Server Manager. To do this, click **Start**, select **Administrative Tools** and then select **Server Manager**.

In the left navigation pane, expand **Roles**, then right-click **Web Server (IIS)** and select **Add Role Services**, as shown in Figure 7|1.

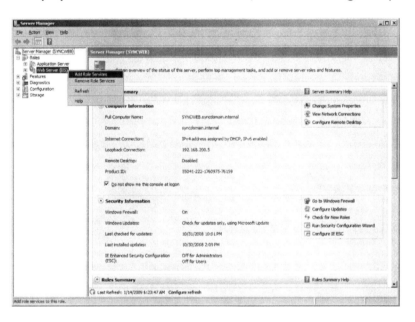

Figure 7|1 > Server Manager

On the **Select Role Services** pane, scroll down to the Management Tools part of the tree view and ensure all the IIS 6 Management Compatibility check boxes are checked, as shown in figure 7|2.

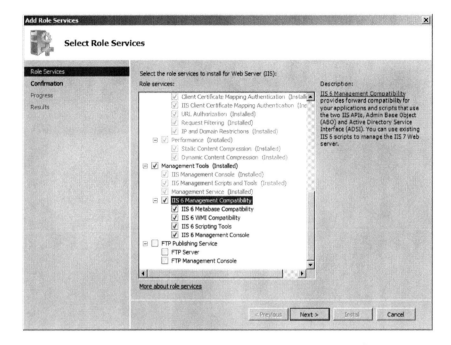

Figure 7|2 > Select Roles Services

Click **Next** from the Select Role Services pane, and then click **Install** at the **Confirm Installations Selections** pane, as shown in Figure 7|3.

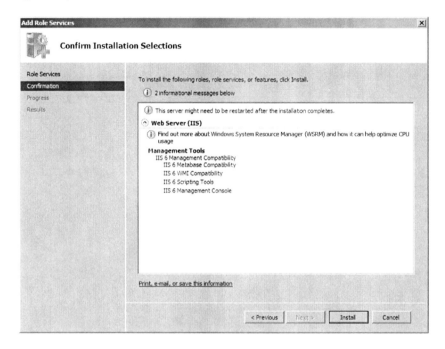

Figure 7|3 > Confirm Installation Selections

Once the installation is completed, as shown in Figure 7|4, click **Close** to leave the Add Role Services wizard.

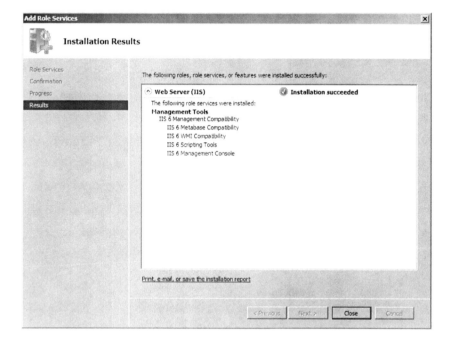

Figure 7|4 > Installation Results

SQL Server 2008 Client Components

Since SSCE replicates its data with SQL Server 2008 over HTTP(S), it's necessary to install the appropriate middleware on IIS. To begin installing the SQL Server 2008 Replication Components, insert your SQL Server 2008 Developer/ Workgroup/ Standard/ Enterprise CD into the IIS server to start the Autorun process. Depending on the current configuration of your IIS server, the SQL Server 2008 Setup may prompt you to install the .NET Framework 3.5 SP1 and a newer version of the Windows Installer as prerequisites. If this prompting occurs, click OK to proceed with these prerequisite installs, which may require a reboot. Once all the prerequisite software has been installed, you will be presented with the **SQL Server Installation Center,** as shown in Figure 7|5. Select **Installation** on the left.

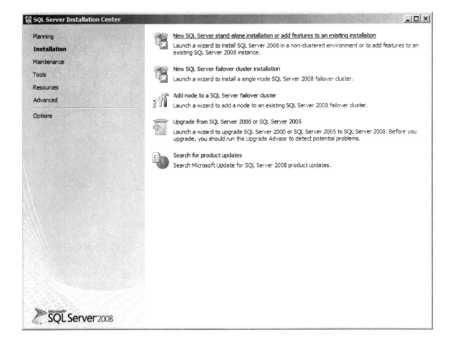

Figure 7|5 > SQL Server Installation Center

Clicking on the **New SQL Server stand-alone installation or add features to an existing installation** hyperlink will bring up the **Setup Support Rules** screen, as shown in Figure 7|6.

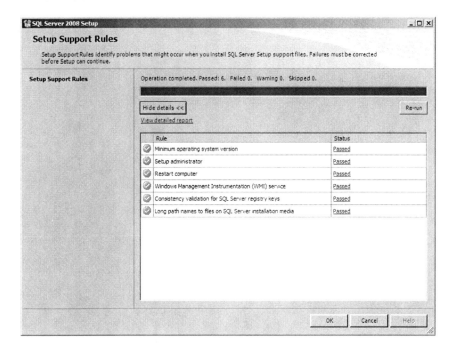

Figure 7|6 > Setup Support Rules

Assuming all the rules receiving a passing grade, click **OK** to bring up the **Product Key** screen, shown in Figure 7|7.

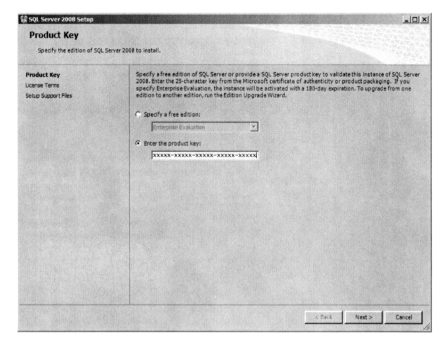

Figure 7|7 > Product Key

Either specify a free edition for a 120-day trial or enter your product key and click **Next**.

On the **License Terms** screen, shown in Figure 7|8, check the **I accept the license terms** check box and click **Next**.

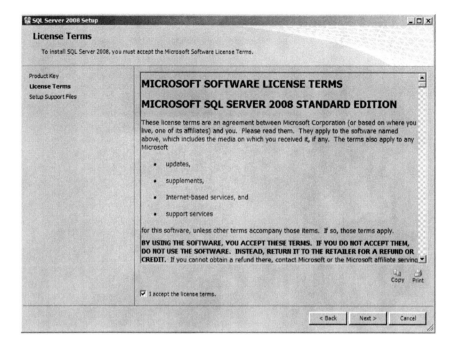

Figure 7|8 > License Terms

The **Setup Support Files** screen, shown in Figure 7|9, displays a list of all the features SQL Server needs to install in order to proceed forward.

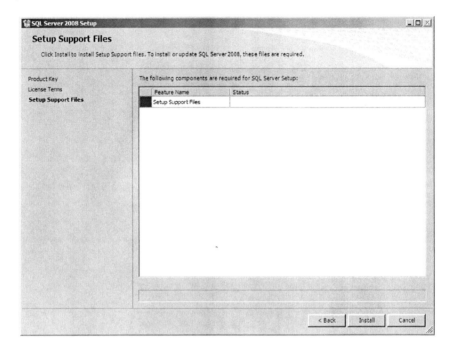

Figure 7|9 > Setup Support Files

Click **Install**.

The **Setup Support Rules** screen, shown in Figure 7|10, displays the status of all the rules after the setup support files have been installed. As you might imagine, we're trying to avoid failure here. Click **Next** when all operations are complete.

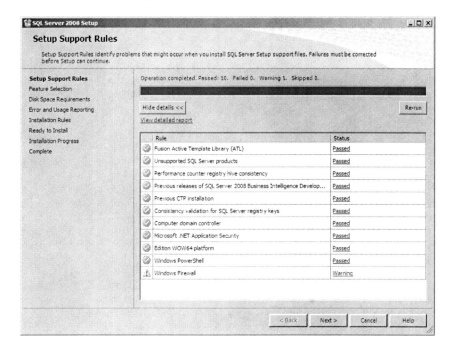

Figure 7|10 > Setup Support Rules

On the **Feature Selection** screen, shown in Figure 7|11, check the
Client Tools Connectivity check box and click **Next**.

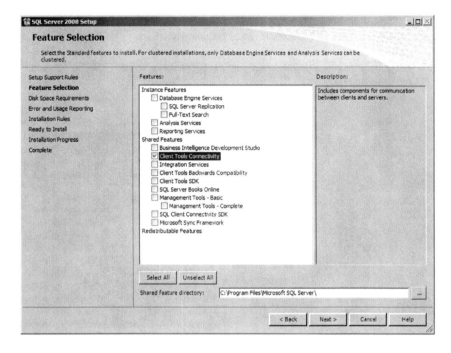

Figure 7|11 > Feature Selection

The **Disk Space Requirements** screen, shown in Figure 7|12, tells you how much space is required on the various drives where you might be installing SQL Server components. It also checks to make sure your server actually has the necessary space. If you get the green check mark, proceed forward by clicking **Next**.

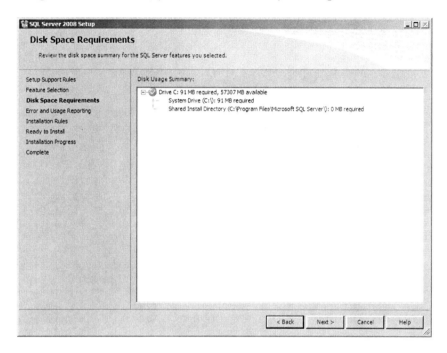

Figure 7|12 > Disk Space Requirements

The **Error and Usage Reporting** screen, shown in Figure 7|13, gives you the opportunity to send usage data and error reports to Microsoft. Opt in or opt out and click **Next**.

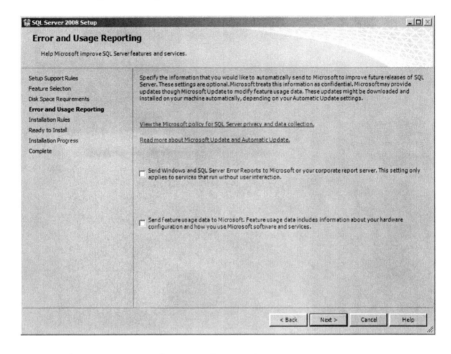

Figure 7|13 > Error and Usage Reporting

The **Installation Rules** screen, shown in Figure 7|14, runs a quick test to determine if any installation processes will be blocked. If everything passes, click **Next**.

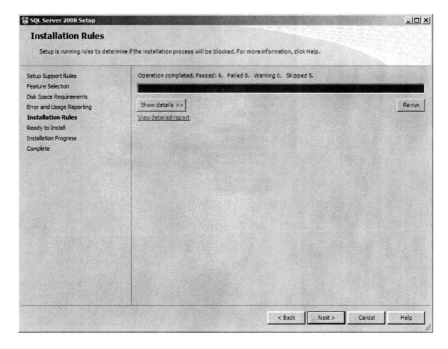

Figure 7|14 > Installation Rules

The **Ready to Install** screen, shown in Figure 7|15, basically displays all the choices you've made throughout the wizard. Review those choices and if you're satisfied, click **Install**.

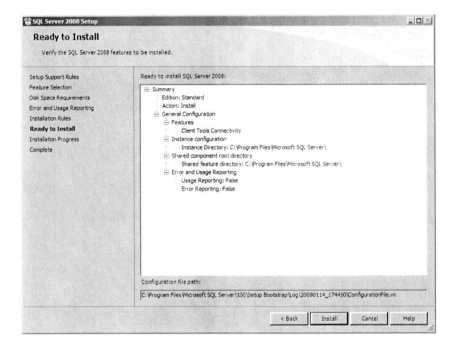

Figure 7|15 > Ready to Install

The **Installation Progress** screen, shown in Figure 7|16, displays a progress bar plus status text to let you know how your installation is proceeding. When the setup is completed with a status of **Success**, click **Next**.

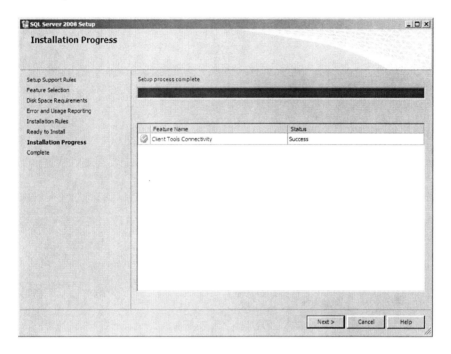

Figure 7|16 > Installation Progress

When everything is finished, you'll be presented with the
Complete screen, as shown in Figure 7|17. Click **Close**.

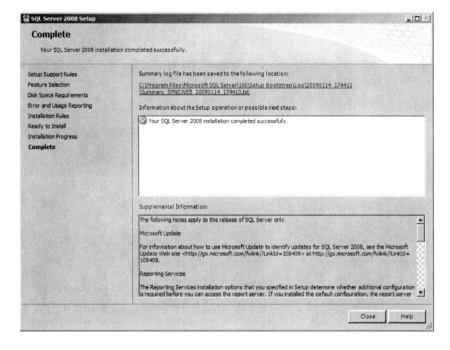

Figure 7|17 > Complete

SQL Server Compact 3.5 SP1 Server Tools

The Microsoft SQL Server Compact 3.5 Service Pack 1 Server Tools install the replication components that IIS needs for the synchronization of data between SQL Server 2005/2008 on the server side and SQL Server Compact 3.0/3.1/3.5/3.5 SP1 on the client side. These tools can be found at http://www.microsoft.com/downloads/details.aspx?displaylang=en&FamilyID=fa751db3-7685-471b-ac31-f1b150422462. A new feature of the SSCE 3.5 SP1 Server Tools is that they now support x64 servers as well as x86. Make sure you download the correct 32- or 64-bit MSI file, appropriate for your IIS server.

Keep in mind that ASP.NET, ISAPI, Security, IIS 6 Management Compatibility components, and the SQL Server Client Tools Connectivity feature must be installed before you begin the installation of the SSCE 3.5 SP1 Server Tools. If everything is ready to go, double click the MSI file you just downloaded to get started.

A wizard is launched and the **Welcome to the Microsoft SQL Server Compact 3.5 SP1 Server Tools Setup** screen is displayed, as shown in Figure 7|18. Click **Next**.

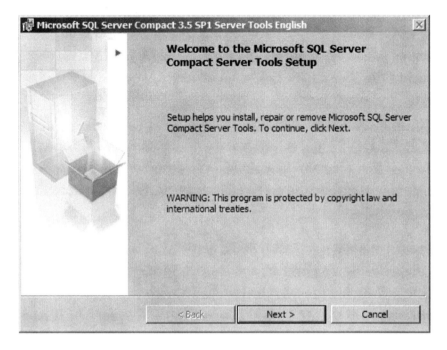

Figure 7|18 > Server Tools Setup

On the **License Agreement** screen, shown in Figure 7|19, select **I accept the terms in the license agreement**, and click **Next**.

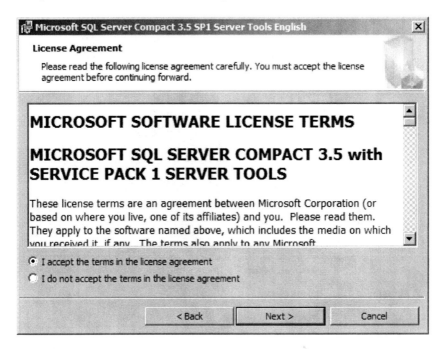

Figure 7|19 > License Agreement

The **System Configuration Check** screen, shown in Figure 7|20, performs a quick check on your server to ensure that all necessary components of the **Server Tools** are properly installed and configured. If the five checks are successful, click **Next**.

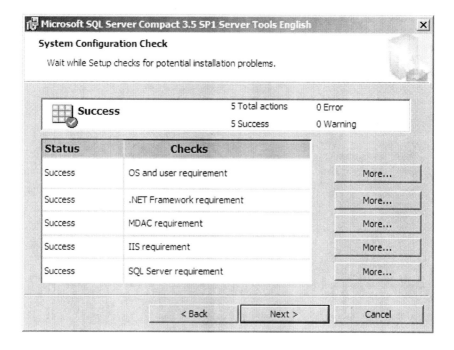

Figure 7|20 > System Configuration Check

The **Microsoft SQL Server Version** screen shows you which version of SQL Server you can synchronize with, as shown in Figure 7|21. It also shows you the installation path where the SSCE Server Agent ISAPI DLL and Log files will ultimately reside. The path to these folders ultimately maps to IIS Virtual Directories. For best disk I/O performance with the .IN, .OUT, and .LOG files that are created, I recommend you click **Browse** and change your installation path to an installed disk drive or array, other than the one where Windows Server is installed. Preferably, this would be an unshared LUN configured for RAID 10, or it could just be your D:\ drive. Click **Next**.

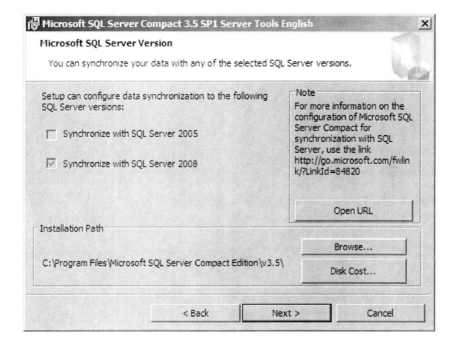

Figure 7|21 > Microsoft SQL Server Version

The **Ready to Install the Program** screen, shown in Figure 7|22, indicates that the Setup is ready to begin the installation, based on your choices. Click **Install** to begin the process, or **Back** if you need to alter your configuration.

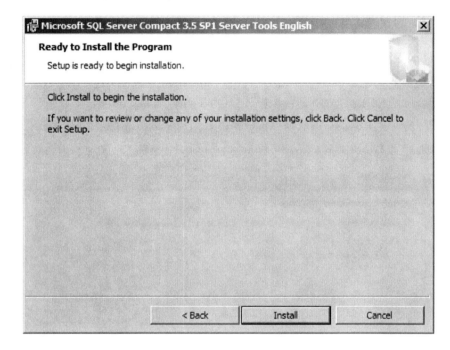

Figure 7|22 > Ready to Install the Program

After displaying a progress dialog during the installation process, the **Completing the Microsoft SQL Server Compact Server Tools Setup** screen is displayed, as shown in Figure 7|23. Click **Finish** to complete the installation.

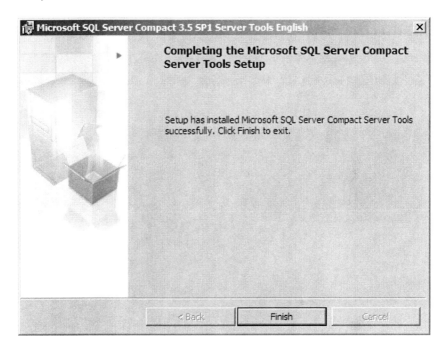

Figure 7|23 > Completing the Server Tools Setup

Configure Web Synchronization Wizard.

Now that the SQL Server 2008 Client Components and the SQL Server Compact 3.5 SP1 Server Tools are installed on IIS, it's time to configure Web Synchronization to create a virtual directory and set proper folder permissions for Subscriber access. From the **Start** menu, select **All Programs | Microsoft SQL Server Compact 3.5 | Configure Web Synchronization Wizard**, as shown in Figure 7|24.

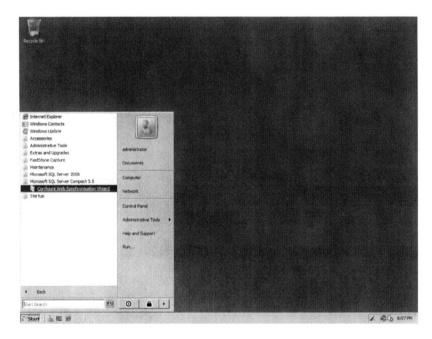

Figure 7|24 > Launch Configure Web Synchronization Wizard

This will bring up the **Welcome to the Configure Web Synchronization Wizard** screen, as shown in Figure 7|25. Click **Next**.

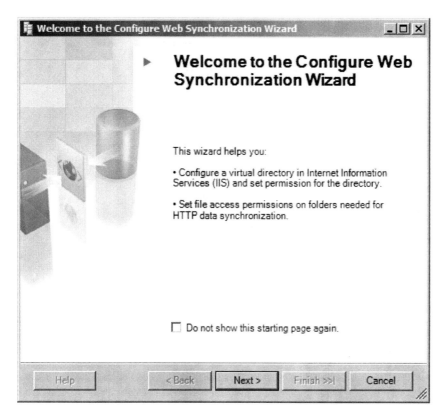

Figure 7|25 > Configure Web Synchronization Wizard

On the **Subscriber Type** screen, select **the SQL Server Compact Edition** radio button, as shown in Figure 7|26, then click **Next**.

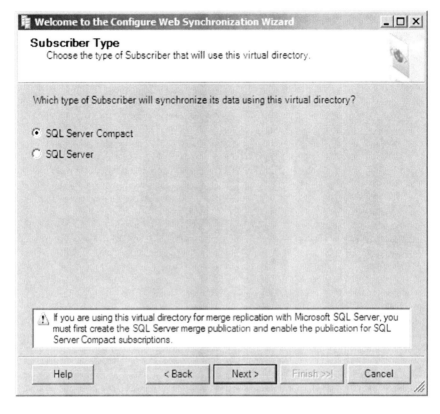

Figure 7|26 > Subscriber Type

On the **Web Server** screen, type in the name of the local computer in the **Enter the name of the computer running IIS** text box, as shown in Figure 7|27, if it's not already displayed. Next, select the **Create a new virtual directory** radio button. In the tree view at the bottom, expand **SYNCWEB (local computer)**, **Web Sites** folder, and select **Default Web Site**. Click **Next**.

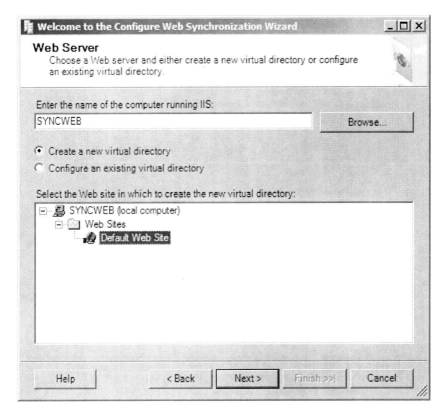

Figure 7|27 > Web Server

The **Virtual Directory Information** screen is where you specify an alias and a path for your new virtual directory. In the **Alias** text box, type in **SSCE** and leave the **Path** text box unchanged (hopefully pointing to another disk drive array), as shown in Figure 7|28. When you click **Next**, you'll be prompted to create a new folder. Click **Yes**. Directly after that, you'll be asked if you want to copy and register the SQL Server Compact Server Agent. Click **Yes**.

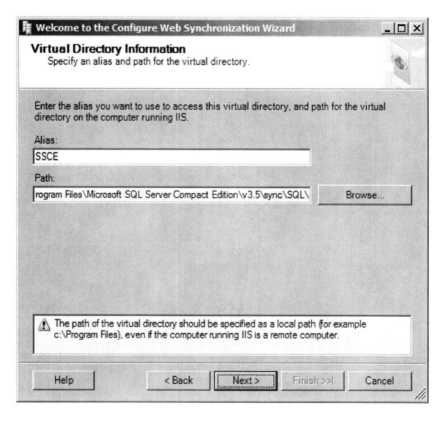

Figure 7|28 > Virtual Directory Information

The **Secure Communications** screen allows you to configure Secure Sockets Layer (SSL) encrypted communications between the mobile SSCE database and the IIS virtual directory you are currently creating. If you have a certificate installed on your IIS server that you obtained from a certificate authority, you can require that all Subscribers use SSL to connect. If you don't have a server certificate installed, the option **not** to use SSL will be pre-selected with all other options grayed out, as shown in Figure 7|29. Whatever you do, don't forget to use SSL when you put your Merge Replication system into production. It's critical that you keep your data and credentials secure as they travel across wired and wireless networks. Click **Next**.

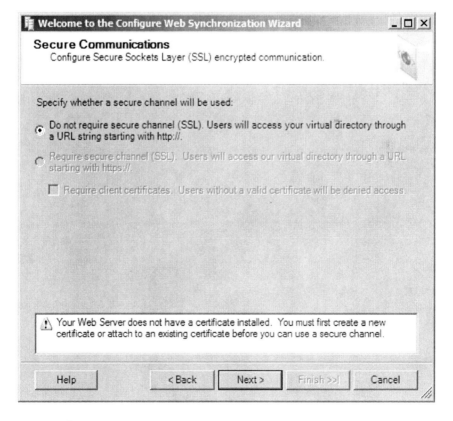

Figure 7|29 > Secure Communications

The **Client Authentication** screen is where you specify the type of authentication that mobile Subscribers will use when they access the virtual directory. Always select the second option, where clients are authenticated and will therefore have to present a User Name and Password to the web server, as shown in Figure 7|30. Click **Next**.

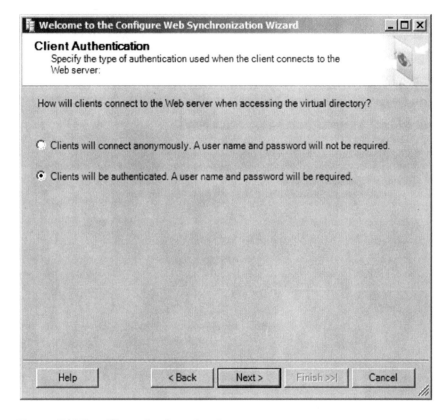

Figure 7|30 > Client Authentication

When you arrive at the **Authenticated Access** screen, you will be presented with a number of ways to authenticate the client credentials that the Subscribers will be passing to the web server. Uncheck **Integrated Windows authentication** and check **Basic authentication,** because this is the option most likely to work across multiple Internet, Intranet, firewall, and proxy scenarios. You will notice that the previously grayed-out **Default Domain** and **Realm** text boxes are now available to you. Since IIS must access the Active Directory to authenticate the User Names, Passwords, and Group memberships of Subscribers trying to replicate with SQL Server, enter your network Domain name in the **Default Domain** text box, as shown in Figure 7|31. Click **Next**.

Figure 7|31 > Authenticated Access

The **Directory Access** screen is where you specify which Domain users and groups can have access to the virtual directory you are creating. Since the **Group or user names** list box is empty, click **Add**, as shown in Figure 7|32.

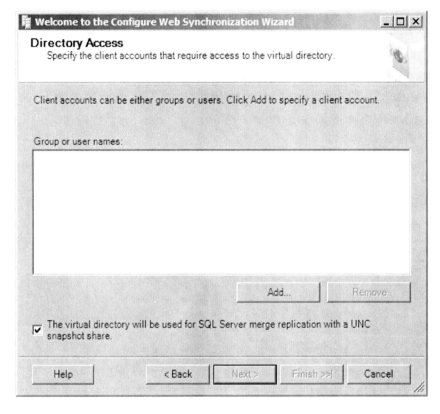

Figure 7|32 > Directory Access

In the **Select Users or Groups** dialog box, click the Object Types button, check the Groups check box and then click **OK**. Next, click the **Locations** button and in the **Locations** dialog, expand the **Entire Directory** node, select **syncdomain.internal** and click **OK**. Type **SyncGroup** in the **Enter the object name to select** text box and then click the **Check Names** button, as shown in Figure 7|33. If the group name is confirmed by displaying the full user name, then click **OK**.

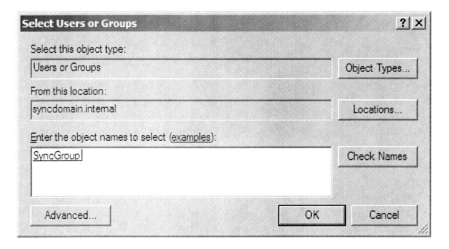

Figure 7|33 > Select Users or Groups

This will add the Domain group to the screen, shown in Figure 7|34. Ensure that the check box at the bottom, specifying that you will access the Snapshot via a UNC share, is checked and click **Next**.

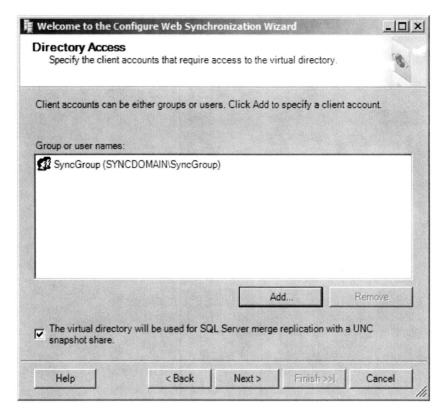

Figure 7|34 > Directory Access

The **Snapshot Share Access** screen is where you specify the location of the Snapshot share on which to set access permissions. You must have administrator privileges for the computer on which the share is located to accomplish this task. In the **Share** text box, enter **\\SYNCPUBLISHER\Snapshot**, as shown in Figure 7|35. Click **Next**. If you get a **Warning** dialog box saying that the **Snapshot** share is empty, click **Yes** to continue.

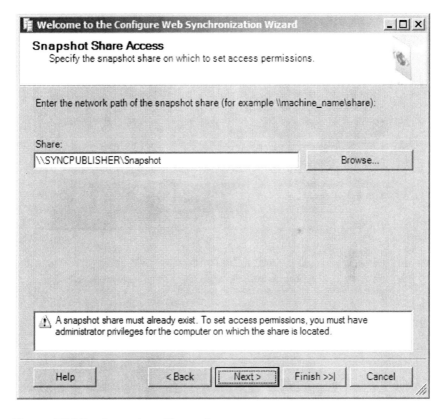

Figure 7|35 > Snapshot Share Access

On the **Complete the Wizard** screen, as shown in Figure 7|36, review the actions to be executed and if they are correct, click **Finish**. If there are any discrepancies, click **Back** to return to earlier screens to fix the problems. Clicking **Finish** starts the process of creating your virtual directory.

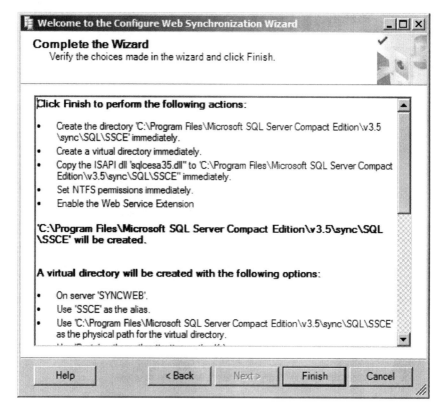

Figure 7|36 > Complete the Wizard

The **Configure Web Synchronization** screen displays the progress of creating the virtual directory, copying the ISAPI DLL, and setting various directory, agent, and share permissions, as shown in Figure 7|37. If all nine actions are successful, click **Close**.

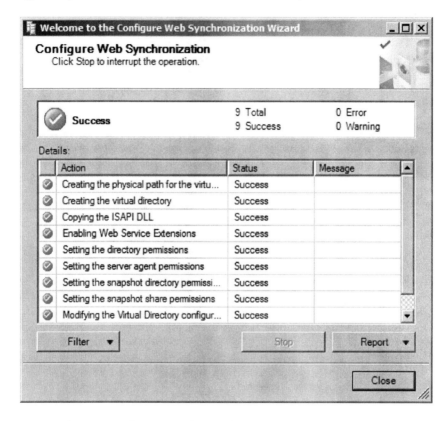

Figure 7|37 > Configure Web Synchronization

Keep in mind that you can rerun the **Web Synchronization Wizard** any time to either add new virtual directories or modify the attributes of existing ones.

Test Web Synchronization.

Now that your middleware is configured on IIS, it's a good idea to test your installation to ensure that it's working before proceeding. Launch **Internet Explorer** and, from the **Address Bar** at the top, enter http://syncweb/ssce/sqlcesa35.dll and press **Enter**. If your Basic authentication was configured correctly, you should be prompted with a **Connect to syncweb.syncdomain.internal** dialog box asking for your **User name** and **Password,** as shown in Figure 7|38. Type **SYNCDOMAIN\syncuser** in the **User name** combo box and **P@ssw0rd** in the **Password** text box, then click **OK**.

Figure 7|38 > Connect to syncweb

If all goes well and the ISAPI DLL is reachable, you will be presented with a web page that reads **Microsoft SQL Server Compact Server Agent**, as shown in Figure 7|39. When deploying this solution to a device, you should also try this test from **Internet Explorer Mobile** on actual Windows Mobile devices. Otherwise, test it from the desktop version of Internet Explorer on desktops, laptop, tablets and Netbooks over the wireless network you intend to use in order to ensure everything works.

Figure 7|39 > Configure Web Synchronization

To get even more comprehensive information about the health of the Server Agent, type http://syncweb/ssce/sqlcesa35.dll?diag in the **Address Bar** at the top of Internet Explorer and press **Enter** to display the **SQL Server Compact Server Agent Diagnostics** page, as shown in Figure 7|40.

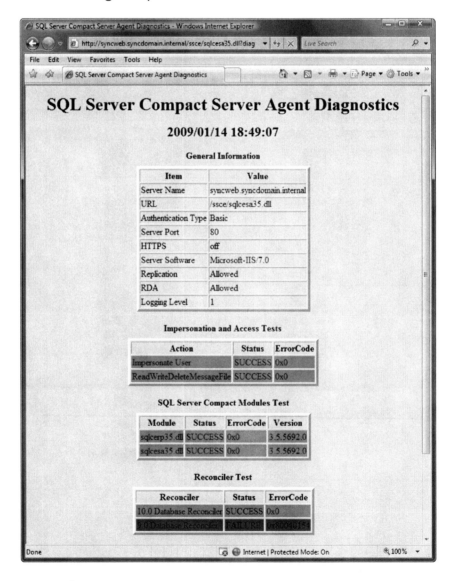

Figure 7|40 > Agent Diagnostics

The first table at the top gives you some obvious information; you're probably already aware of this because it reflects how you set up the web server. The next three tables are more important and relate the success or failure of their respective tests, via green or red indicators.

The **Impersonation and Access Tests** table reflects whether or not the Server Agent was able to impersonate **SYNCDOMAIN\syncuser**, as well as if this user has sufficient access rights to the content folder, via NTFS permissions. If both table rows are displayed in green, then you're in good shape.

The **SQL Server Compact Modules Test** table tells you whether or not the server components were installed and registered properly. The SQLCERP35.DLL file in the first row is the Replication Provider and the SQLCESA35.DLL file in the second row is the Server Agent. Both rows must show up in green in order for your system to work.

The **Reconciler Test** tables displays information about the proper installation and registration of the two possible SQL Server Reconcilers that might be available to you. In the first row, the **10.0 Database Reconciler** refers to SQL Server 2008 and must be green in order for the system described in this book to work. The second row shows the **9.0 Database Reconciler**, which refers to SQL Server 2005. I would expect this row to show up in red since you didn't install support for this database and it isn't used in this book.

Once your servers are in production, you can retrieve real-time statistics about the Server Agent by typing http://syncweb/ ssce/sqlcesa35.dll?stats in the **Address Bar** at the top of Internet Explorer and pressing **Enter** to display the **SQL Server Compact Server Agent Statistics** page, as shown in Figure 7|41.

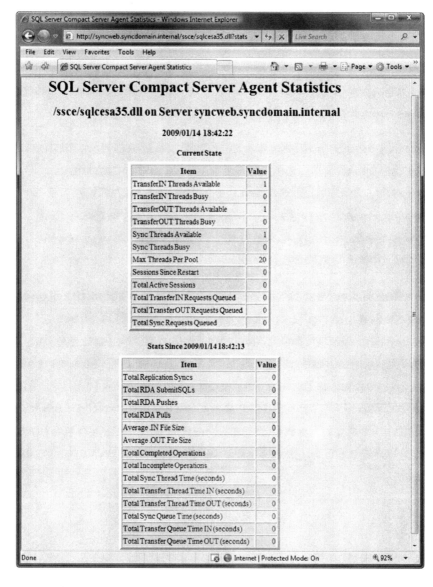

Figure 7|41 > Agent Statistics

This web page displays a wealth of information that gives you a good glimpse of what's going on under the hood. The table on the top, **Current State**, tells you what's occurring at the instant you open the page; and the table at the bottom, **Stats Since…**, gives you a summary of activity from the last fifteen minutes.

The **Current State** table gives you the following real-time information (just keep hitting the refresh button):

- **TransferIN Threads Available**: This is the number of threads available to transfer data from a device to the server, and will grow from one up to the value set in the Max_Threads_Per_Pool registry value (which I'll cover later).
- **TransferIN Threads Busy**: This is the number of threads currently transferring data from devices to the server.
- **TransferOUT Threads Available**: This is the number of threads available to transfer data from the server to the devices and grows from one up to the value set in the Max_Threads_Per_Pool registry value.
- **TransferOUT Threads Busy**: Much like TransferIN Threads Busy, but refers to the number of threads currently transferring data from the server back to the devices.
- **Sync Threads Available**: This is the number of threads available to call the Synchronize() method; that number grows from one up to the value set in the Max_Threads_Per_Pool registry value.
- **Sync Threads Busy**: This is the number of threads currently in the middle of a Synchronize() operation with SQL Server.
- **Max Threads Per Pool**: Using a default value of 20, this is the value found in the Max_Threads_Per_Pool registry

setting. This means that, by default, the **TransferIN** thread pool gets 20 threads, the **TransferOUT** pool get another 20 threads, and the **Sync** pool gets the remaining 20 threads. That's a whopping 60 threads! I wonder how many processors you're going to need on your web server to handle all those threads efficiently? I will show you how to tame this potential thread mania, via the Registry.

- **Sessions Since Restart:** This is the number of sync operations that have occurred since the web server was last rebooted.
- **Total Active Sessions:** Number of sync + data transfer operations that are currently in progress, or waiting in queues.
- **Total Transfer Requests Queued:** This is the number of data transfer requests that are waiting in the queue until a transfer thread becomes available.
- **Total Sync Requests Queued:** This is the number of sync requests waiting in the queue until a sync thread becomes available.

The **Stats Since (whatever time and date)** table summarizes up to 15 minutes of data and includes the following metrics:

- **Total Replication Syncs:** This is the number of replication merges performed.
- **Total RDA SubmitSQLs:** Don't care.
- **Total RDA Pushes:** Still don't care.
- **Total RDA Pulls:** Buy a book on RDA if you truly care.
- **Average .IN File Size:** Average size in bytes of the .IN files that represents the message data sent by the device.

- **Average .OUT File Size**: Average size in bytes of the .OUT files that represents the message data sent from the server.
- **Total Completed Operations**: The number of Synchronize() method calls completed.
- **Total Incomplete Operations**: The number of Synchronize() method calls that started, but didn't finish.
- **Total Sync Thread Time (seconds)**: The total amount of time that all sync threads took to finish their sync operations.
- **Total Transfer Thread Time IN (seconds)**: The total amount of time needed to send data to the server.
- **Total Transfer Thread Time OUT (seconds)**: The total amount of time needed to send data to the devices.
- **Total Sync Queue Time (seconds)**: The total time that device sync requests wait for a sync thread to become available so that a sync operation can begin with the server.
- **Total Transfer Queue Time IN (seconds)**: The total time the device waits in the queue for an available transfer thread to send data to the server.
- **Total Transfer Queue Time OUT (seconds)**: The total time the device waits in the queue for an available transfer thread to send data to the device.

Performance Tuning

I find this tier of the architecture to be one of the biggest bottlenecks in the system. I'm not saying that IIS is the problem though. My testing has shown that it's clear that the Server Agent ISAPI DLL becomes overwhelmed long before IIS is even breaks a sweat. The DLL juggles 3 different thread pools that deal with the SQL Reconciler, as well as the reading and writing of .IN and .OUT files. It's also reading from the Snapshot share on the Distributor and talking to the Publisher while writing out a log file, as well. The big picture here is that even though SQL Server's binary Merge Replication protocol is fast and efficient, you can't help but take a performance hit when you convert it into something that will run over HTTP(S), upon arriving at the IIS tier of the infrastructure. It's the tradeoff we have to make in order to allow mobile devices roaming around the Internet to sync with SQL Server behind the firewall. It's a great tradeoff because the reading and writing of the Replication Session Control Blocks (RSCB) represent small amounts of data moving to and from SSCE on your device. Because of these small blocks, Merge Replication can sync large databases to small, limited-memory devices without overwhelming their working set or causing Out-of-Memory errors. It's also the reason that a sync operation that's been interrupted by a network dropout can resume where it left off when the network returns. The reading and writing of these RSCBs to the drives of your IIS servers means that your devices have a loosely-coupled staging area at the edge of your network that increases the reliability of each sync, as opposed to having SSCE and SQL Server synchronously replicating with each other directly.

Earlier in this chapter, I recommended that instead of just creating your virtual directory for the Server Agent on the C:\ drive, you should utilize a second drive or drive array. With all of the file I/O the ISAPI DLL performs, I don't want it competing with the operating system disk where Windows Server is installed. So at a minimum, add an extra drive to your IIS box. For even better performance, utilize an unshared LUN on a Storage Area Network (SAN) or a Direct Attached Storage (DAS) array with 15,000 RPM Serial Attach SCSI (SAS) drives in a RAID 0 or 10 configuration. A RAID 0 striped array will give you great performance, while a RAID 10 array will provide fault tolerance for your .IN and .OUT files, via disk mirroring. As solid state drives (SSD) get cheaper, you may want to look at them as a faster, more reliable replacement for spinning disk drives.

The Windows Server 2008 that hosts IIS should run at least a dual core processor with 2 GB of RAM. An inexpensive 1U pizza-box rack server will do just fine, or you can go with the blade option. Unlike with the SSCE 3.1 Server Tools, the new tools can be 32- or 64-bits. That being said, I'll never have you equipping a server with enough RAM to warrant a 64-bit memory area. To boost network performance and support Network Load Balancing, make sure your server uses 2 Gigabit Ethernet cards. Following these hardware recommendations should allow you to comfortably support 200 concurrently queued Subscribers per IIS server. Keep in mind that increasing the amount of RAM or the number of CPUs doesn't mean you can push more users through the IIS server. This hardware configuration, when combined with the registry settings I'm about to share with you, is designed to create the perfect balance of performance and scalability. Supporting more than 200 concurrently queued Subscribers will require you to scale out, via additional load-balanced servers.

The last configuration information for the IIS server that I want to pass along deals with some registry setting modifications that I want you to make in order to change the SSCE Server Agent's behavior. If you launch the Registry Editor and navigate to *HKLM\Software\ Microsoft\Microsoft SQL Server Compact Edition\v3.5\Transport*, you'll see four registry keys, as shown in Figure 7|42:

- USAGE
- MAX_THREADS_PER_POOL
- MAX_PENDING_REQUESTS
- LOGGING_LEVEL

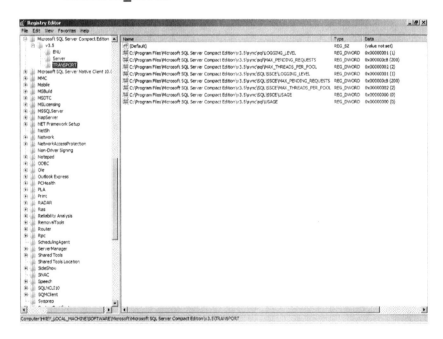

Figure 7|42 > Registry Editor

I'm not terribly concerned with the USAGE key, so let's move along to the MAX_THREADS_PER_POOL key. The default value of this key is 20, which refers to the maximum number of threads that can be used by the 3 thread pools employed by the SSCE Server Agent. There's a thread pool for communicating with the SQL Server Reconciler, one for processing .IN files, and another for processing .OUT files. Keep in mind that the default value of 20 means that up to 60 threads will be dynamically allocated inside an IIS worker process in order to sync data between SSCE and SQL Server 2008. Not only would flooding your IIS server with enough concurrent Subscribers to utilize all 60 threads overwhelm the SQL Server Reconciler, but all the thread context switching would bring IIS to its knees. Since the theme of this book is "less is more," I want you to change the MAX_THREADS_PER_POOL registry key to just 2. While this might sound counterintuitive to people who think more is better, fewer threads equals a more relaxed system and better performance. The setting of 2 matches the 2 CPU cores and 2 GB of RAM installed on your server. It also aligns with the notion that we use one IIS server for every 2 GB of RAM and (2 CPU cores – 2) found in the SQL Server Publisher. Keep in mind that IIS is your gatekeeper to SQL Server, and allowing 20 Subscribers per IIS box to sync at a time would only increase the level of locking and blocking inside the database, ultimately slowing performance. While limiting the number to 2 sounds like a recipe for getting less done for fewer Subscribers, in fact the opposite is true. One last thing: using a Quad-core IIS server with 4 GB of RAM will give you better performance, but it doesn't mean you can increase the thread level to 4. Instead, I encourage you to create 2 virtualized instances of IIS, using Hyper-V to better utilize the resources on your server. Each virtual machine should get 2 cores and 2 GB of RAM.

The MAX_PENDING_REQUEST registry key has a default value of 500. This means that the Server Agent will queue up to 500 concurrent Subscriber requests until a free thread becomes available to perform work. In other words, if more than 500 subscribers try to connect to a single IIS server; subsequent subscribers will get the following message and will need to try again later:

> Error Code: 80004005
>
> Message: A SQL Server Compact Server Agent queue is full and can take no further requests. Try again later.
>
> Minor Err: 28004

Having 500 simultaneous connections to IIS while the Server Agent is trying to read and write .IN and .OUT files, plus communicate with SQL Server, is too much of a burden and performance will suffer. Therefore, I want you to reduce the MAX_PENDING_REQUEST registry key value to 200. This number ensures that you never have more than 200 concurrently queued Subscribers connected to the Server Agent, waiting for a free thread to sync data. This maps to having IIS support 100 concurrently queued Subscribers per CPU core and aligns exactly the same way with the SQL Server Publisher. This is all good, but I want you to go a step further in limiting the number of connections. You can conserve server memory, prevent denial of service attacks, save bandwidth, and relieve the Server Agent of ever having to deal with too many Subscribers by limiting connections globally at the IIS level. By default, IIS is set to allow an unlimited number of connections to the server, which runs counter to our "less is more" theme for this book. Therefore, I want you to set the IIS Connection Limits property to 200. To accomplish this, launch the Windows Server 2008 Server Manager and expand **Roles | Web Server (IIS)** and click on **Internet Information Services (IIS) Manger**. In the pane to the right under **Connections**, expand the icon with your **<Server Name> | Sites** and click on **Default Web Site**. In the pane on the far right, click **Limits**. In the **Edit Web Site Limits** dialog, check **Limit number of connections** and type 200 in the text box and click **OK**. From now on, whenever you exceed 200 Subscribers trying to connect to IIS, you'll get the following error message:

> Error Code: 80004005
>
> Message: The IIS service is not available.
>
> Minor Err: 28025
>
> Source: Microsoft SQL Server Compact

Just as I mentioned previously, even if you find yourself with a Quad-core IIS server with 4 GB for RAM, keep your Subscriber limit set to 200.

The final Registry setting I want you to look at is the LOGGING_LEVEL key that is set to a value between 0 and 3, as shown in the table below:

Value	Description
0	No logging
1	Errors
2	Errors + Warnings
3	Errors + Warning + Informational Messages

When you first bring your IIS server online and begin synchronizing in a staging environment, set the LOGGING_LEVEL registry key to 1 so you'll be aware of any errors that might occur. If you're having serious performance or stability problems with your system, set the key to 3 to get verbose diagnostic information regarding each sync. Keep in mind that a setting of 3 creates additional I/O and will contribute to the slowing down of your system. When everything is debugged, tuned and ready to go into production, you might consider setting the key to 0 to disable logging, and thus get greater I/O performance.

Note that whenever you make a change to these registry values, you'll need to restart the IIS service in order for the changes to take effect. This can be accomplished by typing **iisreset** at the command prompt.

The next thing I want to discuss in this performance section is IIS scalability and high-availability. As I mentioned earlier, you will deploy one IIS server for every 200 concurrently queued Subscribers that you want to service. Knowing that you'll have 200 Subscribers queued, and 2 actively synching per box at any one time, makes the math for scaling-out pretty easy. Scaling-out and maintaining high-availability is achieved through the use of a load-balancing solution like Windows Server's built-in Network Load Balancing, or a 3rd party product like BIG-IP from F5. This will ensure that Subscriber traffic is spread out and will never be sent to an unavailable server. All Subscribers on the Internet will point to the load-balancer's Virtual IP cluster address, using a Reverse Proxy to accomplish this. At a processor core level, divide the number of SQL Server Publisher cores by 4 to come up with the number of IIS servers to deploy. In other words, if you have a 16-core SQL Server Publisher, you'll divide the number of cores by 4 to arrive at the number 4. You'll therefore deploy 4 IIS servers to support 800 concurrently queued Subscribers, with 8 actively synching at any given time. Keep in mind that this represents my most conservative recommendation; this is where I want you to start. From there, you should stress test your system and look at CPU, memory, disk I/O, and database locking and blocking to determine if you can bring additional IIS servers online to increase the load on the SQL Server Publisher. Remember, a relaxed system not only scales and performs better, but it's more reliable too. Smooth, reliable operation is critical to your long-term success and it prevents the phone from ringing at the help desk.

To ensure high availability for even the smallest deployments, you should never have fewer than 2 load-balanced IIS servers handling your load. The Replication Session Control Blocks are stateful; therefore you must enable server Affinity on your load-balancer so that once a Subscriber begins a session with a particular Server Agent, it always returns to that IIS server until the synchronization is complete. Stateless and/or round-robin configurations will fail.

You might now be thinking that you need to support thousands, not hundreds of Subscribers. The key considerations are: how many concurrent Subscribers do you need to support at any given time? and how much data are they synchronizing? If only 10% of your total deployed user base needs to sync at any one time and they're only transferring a few KB of data each, then the previous example of supporting 800 concurrently queued Subscribers would support a user base of 8,000 Subscribers. If that same 10% needs to sync 100 KB of data each, then each Subscriber will be connected longer and you face the possibility of overlapping with folks who were going to be synchronizing a little later. This lengthening of time may mean that you now have 20% of your users simultaneously replicating data. This changes the math, since you may have as many as 1,600 concurrently queued Subscribers, meaning you will need to add additional IIS servers and increase SQL Server's memory and cores to get back to the 10% level. Anyway, it's all math, and as long as you ensure that your Subscribers synchronize no more than a few rows of data each time, you should be in good shape in your ability to support tens of thousands of Subscribers.

One last thing on performance; since those initial first syncs can be rather lengthy, depending on the size of the database you need to download, ensure that you always perform initializations over a fast, reliable Wi-Fi network or via an ActiveSync cradle. In the rare case that you find yourself having to perform large database initialization over a slower, unreliable wireless data network, ensure that you set your organization's firewall/proxy timeouts to a higher value so that long-running replications aren't chopped in half. Determine how long it will take to download the database over the network, and boost the inbound TCP timeout.

Summary

As you can see, IIS and the Server Agent are a critical part of the Merge Replication equation, with many different variables to consider. While most of this chapter has been a "how-to" on getting the right bits installed and configured properly, the section on performance tuning is critical to your success for anything larger than a workgroup deployment. If you take seriously my hardware recommendations and Registry modifications, and never build a solution that requires the replication of dozens or hundreds of rows per sync, and don't overwhelm SQL Server with too many concurrent Subscribers, then you should be in great shape.

Chapter 8 > Coding the Subscriber

Chapter Takeaways

The primary purpose of this chapter is to teach you how to write high-performance code, enabling your Windows Mobile or .NET Smart Client application to merge replicate with SQL Server.

When you have a large number of mobile subscribers deployed in a distributed environment, your client-side code needs to proactively address topics like security, replication failures, scheduled replication, maintenance of the subscriber database, and easing the challenges of remote technical support. While we will not cover the full spectrum of SQL Server Compact programming best practices, we will address many of the things you can do as a developer to ensure success over the long-term, with hundreds of subscribers using merge replication deployed in a field environment.

Get the Software

Client application development with SQL Server Compact 3.5 SP1 is facilitated through the use of Visual Studio 2008 SP1. Since the Windows Mobile bits don't ship with Visual Studio 2008 SP1, you'll need to download them manually from http://www.microsoft.com/downloads/details.aspx?FamilyID=fce 9abbf-f807-45d6-a457-ab5615001c8f&DisplayLang=en.

A sample Visual Studio 2008 project demonstrating many of the best practices in this chapter is available for download at:

http://cid-8b9c82da88af61fc.skydrive.live.com/self.aspx/ Public/ContosoMobile.zip.

Developing with SQL Compact and Replication

To enable a .NET client application for SQL Server Compact and to leverage Merge Replication, the first step is always to add a project reference to System.Data.SqlServerCe and choose the correct assembly version for the platform your application targets (Desktop or Windows Mobile).

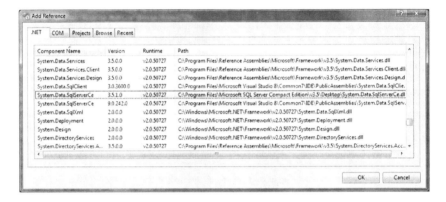

Figure 8|1 > Add Reference

If you are creating a Windows Mobile application, SQL Compact Edition 3.5 SP1 will need to be deployed separately to the mobile device from your application (SQL CE 3.5 is not yet in the ROM of the currently shipping Windows phones).

Be sure to deploy and install the replication CAB (i.e. "sqlce.repl.[phone | ppc].[os].CAB"), as well as the core database CAB file for the platform you are targeting.

Figure 8|2 > Device CABs

If you are targeting a desktop, laptop, tablet or Netbook, you can either require the SQL Server Compact redistributable to be deployed to each Subscriber's computer, or you can simply include the requisite SSSCE DLLs in your project as Content, which makes packaging and deployment simple. Be sure to include the replication DLL in your project, if you choose this option. For more information and advanced deployment techniques such as ClickOnce, see:

http://msdn.microsoft.com/en-us/library/bb219481(SQL.90).aspx

The SqlCeReplication Object

The code to achieve Merge Replication with SQL Server Compact revolves around the SqlCeReplication object. Beyond instantiating this object, setting a few properties, and calling the

Synchronize() method, a deeper dive is important as this object provides you with numerous options which can greatly improve replication performance, the user experience while replicating, and improved support of deployed devices. Figures 8|3 and 8|4 illustrate the SqlCeReplication object required to synchronize with the server configuration created through the first 7 chapters of this book. Following this code sample, I'll cover each of the properties of the SqlCeReplication object in detail.

```csharp
using System.Data.SqlServerCe;

SqlCeReplication _repl = null;

try
{
    //Create the replication object
    _repl = new SqlCeReplication();

    //Assemble the connection string
    _repl.SubscriberConnectionString =
    @"Data Source = \\ContosoMobile.sdf;
    Temp File Max Size = 4091;
    Password = P@ssw0rd;Max Database Size = 4091;
    Max Buffer Size = 4096;Flush Interval = 20;
    Autoshrink Threshold = 10;Default Lock
    Escalation = 100";Default Lock Timeout = 6000;
    Temp File Directory = \\Storage Card;

    //Set Publisher properties
    _repl.PublisherSecurityMode =
    SecurityType.NTAuthentication;
    _repl.Publisher = "SYNCPUBLISHER";
    _repl.PublisherLogin = "SYNCDOMAIN\\syncuser";
    _repl.PublisherPassword = "P@ssw0rd";
    _repl.PublisherDatabase = "ContosoBottling";
    _repl.Publication = "ContosoBottlingPub";
```

Figure 8|3 > SqlCeReplication Code (Part 1)

```
        //Set Internet properties
        _repl.InternetUrl =
        "http://SYNCWEB/ssce/sqlcesa35.dll";
        _repl.InternetLogin = "SYNCDOMAIN\\syncuser";
        _repl.InternetPassword = "P@ssw0rd";
        _repl.ConnectionManager = true;

        //Set Distributor properties
        _repl.Distributor = "SYNCPUBLISHER";
        _repl.DistributorLogin =
        "SYNCDOMAIN\\syncuser";
        _repl.DistributorPassword = "P@ssw0rd";
        _repl.DistributorSecurityMode =
        SecurityType.NTAuthentication;

        //Set Timeout properties
        _repl.ConnectionRetryTimeout = 120;
        _repl.ConnectTimeout = 3000;
        _repl.ReceiveTimeout = 60000;
        _repl.SendTimeout = 1000;

        //Set Subscriber properties
        _repl.Subscriber = "SYNCSUBSCRIBER";
        _repl.HostName = "Darren";
        _repl.CompressionLevel = 6;
        _repl.ExchangeType =
        ExchangeType.BiDirectional

        //Call replication methods
        _repl.Synchronize();
    }
    catch (SqlCeException sqlEx)
    {
        AggregateSSCErrors(sqlEx);
    }
    finally
    {
        //Dispose of Replication object
        if (_repl != null)
        {
            _repl.Dispose();
        }
    }
```

Figure 8|4 > SqlCeReplication Code (Part 2)

SubscriberConnectionString

Parameter	Description
Data Source	File path and name of the local SSCE database.
Temp File Max Size	Maximum size of the temporary database file (in Megabytes). This can be set has high at 4091.
Password	SQL Server Compact database password, which can be up to 40 characters in length. Setting this property enables 128-bit encryption on the database. The password represents the encryption key.
Max Database Size	Maximum size of the database (in Megabytes). This can be set has high at 4091.
Max Buffer Size	The largest amount of memory (in kilobytes) that SSCE can use before it begins flushing changes to disk. Increasing the size of this parameter will boost database performance. Do not set this to anything less than 4096 on the desktop and 1024 on mobile.
Flush Interval	The interval time (in seconds) before all committed transactions are flushed to disk. Setting this interval to a setting higher than the default of 10 seconds can boost database performance but puts uncommitted transactions at risk if you have a hard drive or device failure.
Autoshrink Threshold	Percent of allowable free space in the database file before autoshrink begins. Value of 100 disables autoshrink. The default value is 60.

	Keep your database compact and fast by setting the value to 10.
Default Lock Escalation	The number of locks a transaction will acquire before attempting escalation from row to page or from page to table.

Publisher Properties

Property	Description
PublisherSecurityMode	Can be set to use Windows or SQL Server Authentication. Follow security best practices and always use Windows Authentication.
Publisher	Name of the SQL Server that contains the Publication.
PublisherLogin	Domain name\user name needed to connect to the Publisher.
PublisherPassword	Domain password needed to connect to the Publisher.
PublisherDatabase	Name of the database being published.
Publication	Name of the Publication.

Distributor Properties

Property	Description
Distributor	SQL Server that contains the Distribution database.
DistributorLogin	Domain name\user name needed to connect to the Distributor.
DistributorPassword	Domain password needed to connect to the Distributor.
DistributorSecurityMode	Can be set to use Windows or SQL Server Authentication.

	Follow security best practices and always use Windows Authentication.

Timeout Properties

Property	Description
ConnectionRetryTimeout	Specifies how long (in seconds) the Subscriber will continue to retry sending requests after an established connection has failed. In the event of a network dropout, the data transfer will start where it left off, rather than restarting the whole operation from scratch. High Bandwidth: 30 Medium Bandwidth: 60 Low Bandwidth: 120
ConnectTimeout	Amount of time (in milliseconds) that the Subscriber waits for a connection to the server. High Bandwidth: 3000 Medium Bandwidth: 6000 Low Bandwidth: 12000
ReceiveTimeout	Amount of time (in milliseconds) that the Subscriber waits for the response to a server request. High Bandwidth: 1000 Medium Bandwidth: 3000 Low Bandwidth: 6000
SendTimeout	Amount of time (in milliseconds) that the Subscriber waits to send a request to the server. High Bandwidth: 1000 Medium Bandwidth: 3000 Low Bandwidth: 6000

Web Properties

Property	Description
InternetUrl	The URL needed to connect to the SSC Server Agent.
InternetLogin	Domain name\user name needed to connect to the Server Agent.
InternetPassword	Domain password needed to connect to the SSC Server Agent.

Subscriber Properties

Property	Description
Subscriber	Name of the Subscriber
HostName	A value you set that gets passed to the server to facilitate parameterized queries. This value accepts a string, so if you want to send an integer, don't forget to surround it with quotes and then use the Convert function on the server.
CompressionLevel	Set a value from 0 to 6 to compress the data being transmitted between IIS and the Subscriber. In a high bandwidth scenario, set the value to 0 to disable compression. Set compression to 6 for slow transports like GPRS, EDGE and 1xRTT. Less compression will be needed for EV-DO and HSPDA. Keep in mind that both IIS and your device will take a slight performance hit when compressing and decompressing the data.

SqlCeReplication Methods

Method	Description
AddSubscription	Creates a new anonymous subscription to an existing Publication. The AddOption parameter lets you specify CreateDatabase to create a new mobile database or ExistingDatabase to use a database you already have. CreateDatabase simplifies deployment and can be invaluable in troubleshooting situations.
DropSubscription	Drops the subscription to a Publication. The DropOption parameter lets you specify DropDatabase to delete the local database or LeaveDatabase to delete the replication system tables and columns, but leave the database intact.
ReinitializeSubscription	Marks a Subscription for reinitialization. You need to reinitialize a Subscription whenever you send a different value for the Hostname property or when you change the database schema via T-SQL. The UploadBeforeReinitialize parameter allows you to upload local database changes before reinitializing, if set to True.
Synchronize	Invokes merge replication between the Subscriber and the Publisher. All connections to the local database must be closed before calling this method. The first time you call this method, the

	initial snapshot database is downloaded to the device in small blocks, so as to not overwhelm the available RAM.

Synchronization

Calling Synchronize on the SqlCeReplication object initiates the process of merge replication between SQL Server Compact and the server *synchronously*. You can also replicate *asynchronously* with callback messages and provide your users with visual indication of the progress of the replication, as shown in Figure 8|5 below. A complete implementation is provided with the sample code that accompanies this chapter.

```
IAsyncResult ar = _repl.BeginSynchronize(
    new AsyncCallback(
        this.SyncCompletedCallback),
    new OnStartTableUpload(
        this.OnStartTableUploadCallback),
    new OnStartTableDownload(
        this.OnStartTableDownloadCallback),
    new OnSynchronization(
        this.OnSynchronizationCallback),
    _repl);
```

Figure 8|5 > Asynchronous SqlCeReplication Code

You can leverage this approach to provide the user visual feedback on the progress of replication, like Figure 8|6:

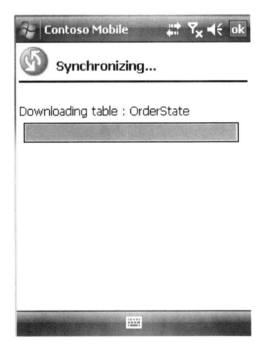

Figure 8|6 > Synchronizing...

A feature of the SqlCeReplication object that can be priceless is the AddSubscription(AddOption.CreateDatabase) approach to dynamically creating the SQL Server Compact database during the synchronization process. I recommend always using this approach as it solves a couple of challenges in deploying and maintaining a large number of distributed mobile clients. If the database can be dynamically created the first time your client application is executed, you no longer have to worry about deploying your application with a "starter" or empty SQL Server

Compact database. After deployment, if significant schema changes occur on the server which cannot be replicated to existing subscribers or, despite all efforts, a Subscriber simply cannot replicate, having the user delete the SQL Server Compact database file and replicate again (creating a fresh database) brings the local database up to the current schema level and often solves difficult replication errors. Don't worry; they can upload any critical data they've captured before starting over.

Be sure to set this option only when the SSCE database does not yet exist or is in need of reinitialization. One other tip: the order in which you set the SqlCeReplication properties also matters; the SubscriberConnectionString must be set before attempting to AddSubscription.

If you are using this approach (and your Help Desk will thank you for doing so), an automatic replication when your application starts up is critical and serves to ensure that the SSCE database will be there for the application after startup.

Note that the ability to dynamically create the entire database at runtime automatically is a feature not available with SQL Server Express Edition Merge Replication.

An important topic often overlooked is *when* and *how often* to synchronize your mobile data to the server. In any situation where users are in the field capturing data throughout the work day, you should attempt to get that valuable data back to the safety of a corporate server as often as possible.

While a "Synch Now" button allowing the end user to initiate Merge Replication is a popular approach, as shown in Figure 8|7, consider an automatic or scheduled replication whenever the application starts (or exits), or based on time since last replication. Remember that coding an automatic synchronization at application startup makes it possible to deploy your application without a starter database, as well as to instruct a user having problems to "delete your SDF file and restart the app".

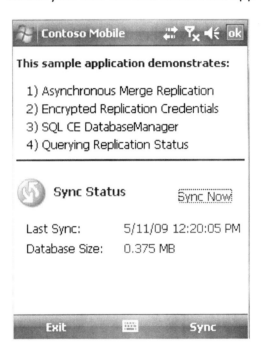

Figure 8|7 > Sync Status

With laptop and tablet applications which are usually connected via high-speed Ethernet or Wi-Fi adapters, the time required to synchronize is often so brief that it is usually a good idea to auto-sync on startup, at shutdown, and perhaps even every X minutes while the user is logged in. For Windows phones or Netbook applications, you have much more to consider. The device's communications capabilities (cellular, WiFi, Bluetooth to a cell phone, and/or cradle), network availability, bandwidth, link quality, and battery life, as well as the user's work environment, all play a factor. A user who drives a delivery truck and is only connected in the motor pool at the beginning and end of every shift is a much different replication scenario than a field sales rep on a HSDPA Windows phone in a large, metro area. Also consider how often the user must download or upload data from the server in order to perform their next task; 8 hours between syncs might cause a field user to miss an assignment or data captured in the field to grow stale, thus affecting back office workflows.

If you decide to synchronize based on how long it has been since the last good synchronization, you can query SQL Server Compact to find out when that last occurred, as shown in Figure 8|8. Tip: be sure to check for the existence of the __sysMergeSubscriptions system table (i.e. query INFORMATION_SCHEMA.TABLES for the table name) before querying it or you will get a SqlCeException.

```
SELECT LastSuccessfulSync FROM
__sysMergeSubscriptions
WHERE Publication = 'ContosoBottlingPub'
```

Figure 8|8 > Last Successful Sync

It is possible, however, for that initial replication to encounter a problem, resulting in a failed attempt. Depending on the cause of this failure, a placeholder SSCE database, 20KB in size, may be created on the client machine, which is effectively useless, as that 20KB database is empty. Always coding defensively, as your application initializes, you should do two things every time:

1) Check for the existence of the SQL Server Compact database before you try to connect to it.
2) Check that the size is greater than 20KB.

```
using System.IO;

//Test to see if database is greater than 20 KB
FileInfo fi = new FileInfo("\\ContosoMobile.sdf");
if (fi.Length > 20480)
{
        //Sync code
}
```

Figure 8|9 > File Size Test

The Help Desk perspective on AddOption.Create database is that if a Subscriber cannot replicate, assuming no new data has been added to the SSCE database since last replication, a simple solution is to exit the app, delete the SDF file, and restart the application.

In scenarios where data may be lost by taking this action, consider creating a "hip-pocket" plan to rescue that data. Examples of SSCE data recovery plans I have used include:

- Add code to your client application to periodically call Verify() and, if needed, Repair() on the SqlCeEngine object.
- Have a SQL Server 2008 Integration Services package standing by, which can post the data to the server. This package can be initiated manually (e.g. user emails you the SDF file) or automatically (e.g. add a "rescue data" option to your application, sending the SDF file to a web service; then logic on the server Verifies, Repairs, and executes the SSIS package).
- Have your application periodically backup the SDF file to an SD card, or other removable media.

While this is a rare event (e.g. on my largest Merge Replication deployment of over 1200 daily Subscribers, it has happened twice in the last year), the first time a Subscriber spends a long shift in the field entering data and then cannot get his work back to the corporate office, you will be well motivated to create a data recovery plan.

Security Considerations

When setting the properties of the SqlCeReplication object, you might be concerned about embedding into your source code the Domain credentials for the web and database servers. Besides the obvious security implications of this practice, having to deploy a new version of the application whenever those credentials change is not manageable for enterprise client deployments.

What if we could encrypt all of the required replication credentials using cryptography that is compatible with Windows, as well as Windows phones, and support any Merge Replication topology? Included in the sample code for this chapter is a project that demonstrates how to achieve this. Leveraging an assembly from the Microsoft Patterns & Practices Team that provides cryptography compatible with both the desktop and Windows Mobile (WM5 and above) platforms, the ReplicationCredentialsGenerator project creates a small binary file called replcred.bin that contains encrypted credentials. This file can then be deployed with your client application, and leveraged at runtime, to securely manage replication credentials. If credentials should ever change, simply deploying a new replcred.bin file to your users is all that is required to accommodate that change.

The **Replication Credentials File Generator,** as shown in Figure 8|10, allows you to enter credentials for the Server Agent on IIS, the Publisher, Distributor, and even a Proxy Server, if need be. Clicking the **Generate Credentials File** button is all it takes to secure your client deployment.

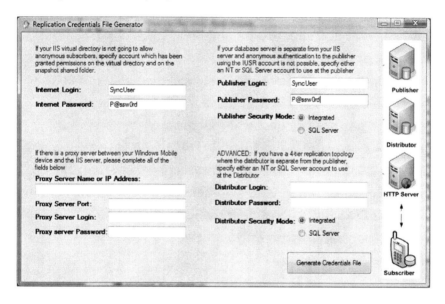

Figure 8|10 > Replication Credentials File Generator

Summary

The key takeaway is to take advantage of all of the parameters and properties that the SqlCeReplication object makes available, giving you finer-grained control over the sync operation. I've really tried to emphasize the use of all of the little-known SubscriberConnectionString parameters. If you don't explicitly set the value of those parameters, you are stuck with default values, which could be inadequate. For instance, the default **Max Database Size** is only 128 MB, which may or may not be a problem if you are working with a large database. The **Max Buffer Size** has a default value of 640 KB, which can cause you to run out of database cursors when replicating more than 100 tables. Boosting the value to at least one, if not several, megabytes can really boost your replication and data manipulation performance, if your device has the free RAM available.

The important properties I try to focus on deal with bandwidth issues. The **CompressionLevel** property gives you an important weapon to use in the mitigation of bandwidth deficiencies. As I describe earlier in the chapter, there's no free lunch when it comes to compression. Using it will help you tremendously over slow networks like GPRS. That being said, your device and web server will use more CPU cycles to compress and decompress the data stream, so take that into account when selecting your hardware. The four timeout properties I describe include: ConnectionRetryTimeout, ConnectTimeout, ReceiveTimeout, and SendTimeout. With each of these properties, I pass along the recommended settings for high, medium and low bandwidth settings, which I hope you will follow when moving your replication system into production.

Lastly, don't assume anything and always test for the existence and size of your local database file before using it. In my experience of stress-testing mobile synchronization in a data center with 2,000 concurrent replicating Subscribers, these simple file I/O tests made a significant difference in boosting the level of reliability in a very chaotic environment.

Merge Replication is great "buy and configure" solution for rapidly mobilizing your organization, whether you're deploying Windows phones, Windows 7 on Netbooks, or Vista on laptops. I sincerely hope I've taken you on a sufficiently deep enough dive to help you take your enterprise to a new level of mobility, where employees are empowered to work anywhere, anytime. Best of luck to you and never be afraid to Go Bold with your solutions!

Appendix A > Network Load Balancing

Appendix Takeaways

As you learned in Chapter 7, IIS is the Internet gateway that links laptops, Netbooks, and Windows phones running SQL Server Compact to SQL Server 2008 in your data center. If you only need to support 200 concurrent Subscribers and don't require high availability, you can stop reading now. On the other hand, if you need to scale out to thousands of Subscribers with a system that's less likely to fail, you might look at some form of clustering.

For a scenario that involves clustering identical IIS servers, the Network Load Balancing (NLB) feature of Windows Server 2008 is an inexpensive way to bring high-availability and scalability to HTTP(S) traffic. This clustering technology distributes traffic across multiple servers using TCP/IP. You can also use this to enhance the availability and scalability of things like FTP, firewalls, proxies, VPNs, and Windows Communication Foundation apps.

NLB uses an NDIS 6.0 network driver to balance the load across all clustered servers from a single Virtual IP Address. If a server fails or is taken offline for maintenance, NLB automatically redistributes the load to the remaining servers. Your servers must each have 2 network cards since NLB uses the second NIC to maintain a heartbeat connection with all the other servers in the cluster.

Now that you know how it works, let's get it installed and configured.

Network Load Balancing Feature

In order to get Network Load Balancing to work properly on Windows Server 2008 and IIS 7, you need to install the Network Load Balancing Tools, via the Windows Server 2008 Server Manager. To do this, click **Start**, select **Administrative Tools** and then select **Server Manager**.

In the left navigation pane, highlight **Features,** as shown in Figure A|1. In the **Features** pane, click **Add Features**.

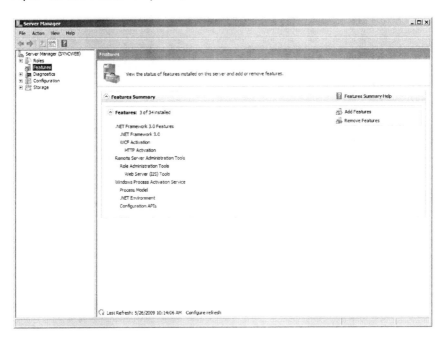

Figure A|1 > Server Manager - Features

On the **Select Features** screen, check **Network Load Balancing,** as shown in figure A|2. Click **Next**.

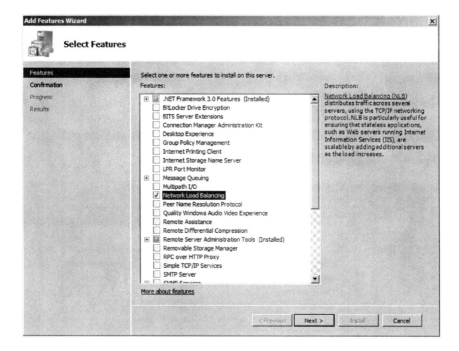

Figure A|2 > Select Features

On the **Confirm Installation Selections** screen, click **Install,** as shown in Figure A|3.

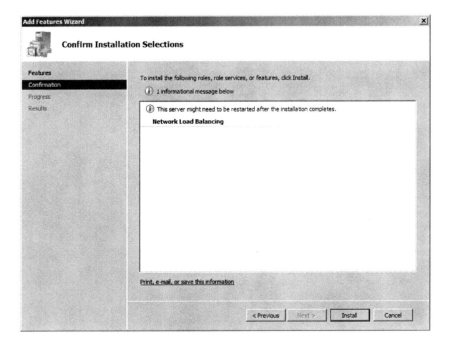

Figure A|3 > Confirm Installation Selections

If all went well, you should see the **Installation succeeded** message, as shown in Figure A|4.

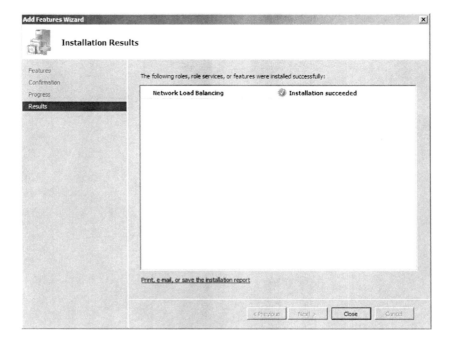

Figure A|4 > Installation Results

With everything installed, click **Start** and select **Administrative Tools | Network Load Balancing Manager,** shown in Figure A|5.

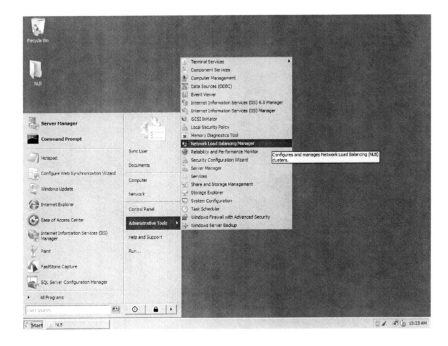

Figure A|5 > Network Load Balancing Manager

Right click on the **Network Load Balancing Clusters** node, as shown in Figure A|6, and select **New Cluster**.

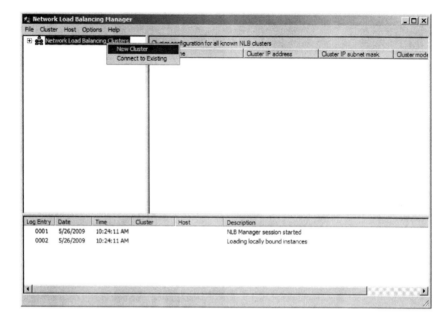

Figure A|6 > New Cluster

On the **Connect** screen, type in the name of the local IIS server and click **Connect,** as shown in Figure A|7.

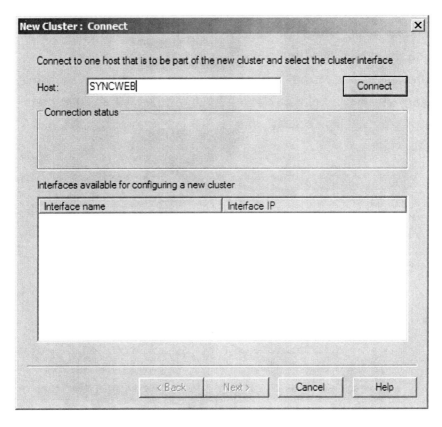

Figure A|7 > Connect

If you connected successfully, the names and IP addresses of the 2 network interface cards on your IIS server will appear, as shown in Figure A|8. Looking at the interfaces that appeared on my virtualized IIS server, the heartbeat NIC is called **NLB Connection** and the primary NIC that receives Internet traffic is called **Loopback Connection**. You can call your network cards anything you want, but it helps to denote the heartbeat NIC to keep them straight. Highlight the NIC that will receive Internet traffic and click **Next**.

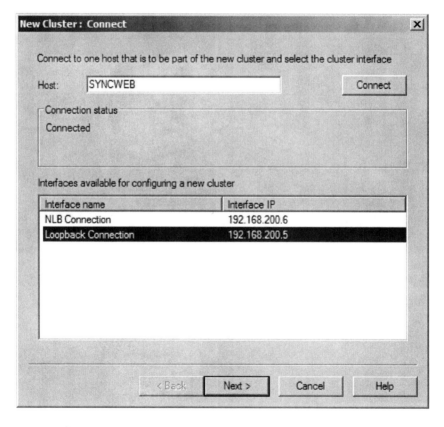

Figure A|8 > Connect

On the Host Parameters screen, the IP address and Subnet mask of the NIC you selected on the previous screen will be displayed as the dedicated IP address, as shown in Figure A|9. The **Priority (unique host identifier)** is set to **1** since it's the first IIS server added to the cluster. All subsequent IIS server will increment upward from there. Leave **Default state** set to **Started** and click **Next**.

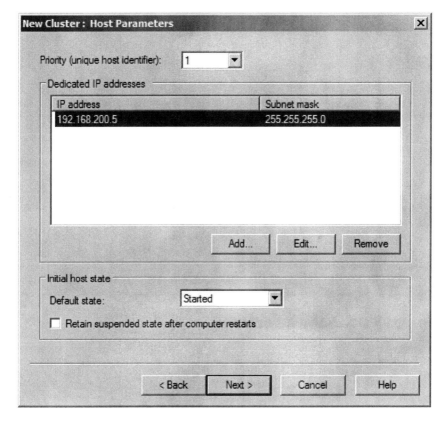

Figure A|9 > Host Parameters

The **Cluster IP Address** screen will show up empty, as shown in Figure A|10. Click **Add.**

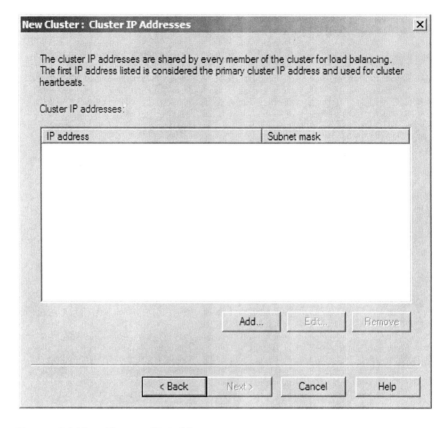

Figure A|10 > Cluster IP Addresses

When the **Add IP Address** dialog pops up, type in the Virtual IP Address (VIP) your cluster will use in the **IPv4 address text box** and then tab down to auto-populate the **Subnet mask** text box, as shown in Figure A|11. Click **OK** to save and close.

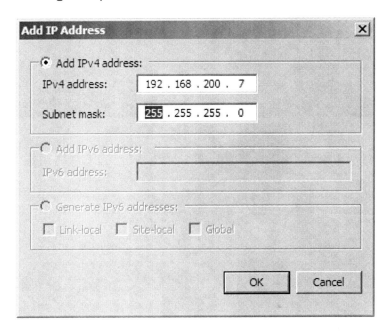

Figure A|11 > Add IP Address

The **Cluster IP Address** screen should now display the VIP you just entered, as shown in Figure A|12. Click **Next**.

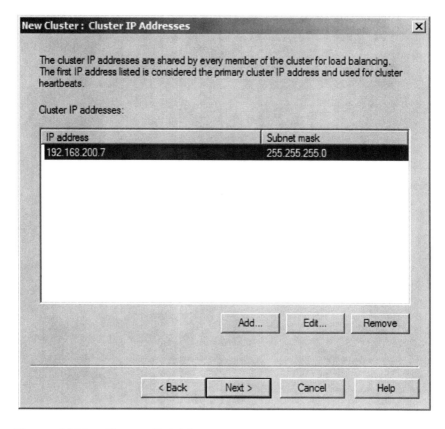

Figure A|12 > Cluster IP Addresses

The **Cluster Parameters** screen will display the VIP, Subnet Mask and MAC Address in the **Cluster IP configuration** section. In the **Full Internet name** text box, enter the Fully Qualified Domain Name (FQDN) that Subscribers will point to when synchronizing, as shown in Figure A|13. Since you have 2 network cards on each of your IIS servers, select **Unicast** in the **Cluster operation mode** section for the most efficient operation. This means that the cluster MAC address will be assigned to the server's NIC, replacing its existing MAC address. Click **Next**.

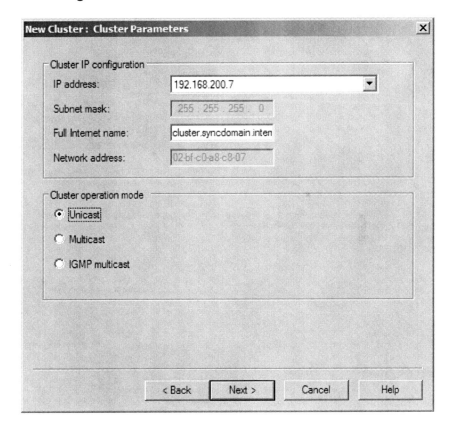

Figure A|13 > Cluster Parameters

On the **Port Rules** screen, the default rule allows traffic from all ports (0 – 65,535) to be handled by all cluster IP addresses, as shown in Figure A|14. Clearly, this rule isn't on anyone's list of security best practices, so I want you to highlight this rule and click **Remove**. Click **Add** in order to create new rules that are appropriate for our needs on IIS.

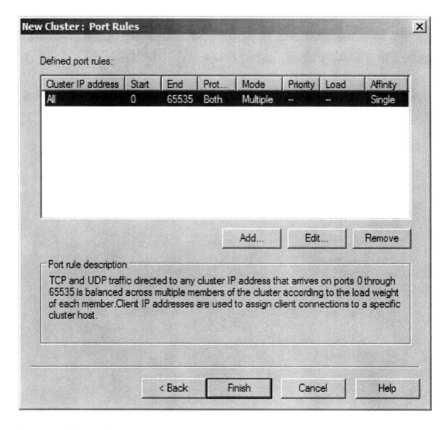

Figure A|14 > Port Rules

The **Add/Edit Port Rule** dialog will appear with its not-so-secure default setting, as shown in Figure A|15.

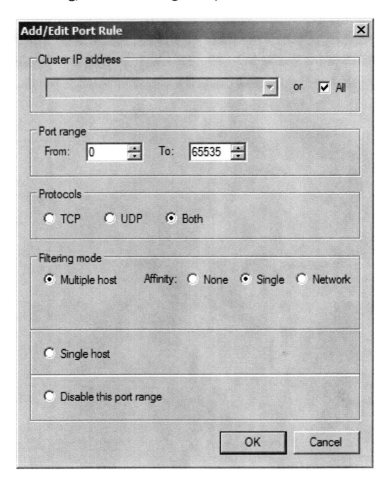

Figure A|15 > Add/Edit Port Rule

Uncheck the **All** check box in the **Cluster IP address** section and the VIP will appear in the combo box, as shown in Figure A|16. Since I want you to create a rule that just lets in HTTP traffic, set the **Port range** to be from 80 to 80 and set the protocol to be **TCP**. Set the **Filtering mode** to be **Mulitple host** with **Single** Affinity to ensure sticky sessions and then click **OK**. To allow SSL traffic, repeat this process with port 443.

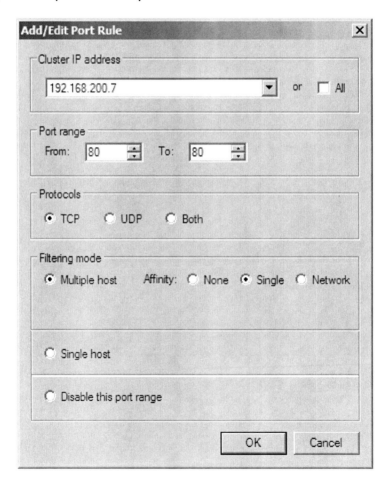

Figure A|16 > Add/Edit Port Rule

One thing to note: traffic that arrives at the Cluster IP address via a port or protocol not covered by a port rule will be handled by the cluster node whose Priority is set to 1. Since you don't want any of your nodes to deal with traffic coming in on ports other than 80 and 443, you still have work to do, so click **Add**.

This time around, uncheck the **All** check box and select your VIP as before. Set the **Port range** to be from 0 to 79 and set the **Protocol** to be **Both**. Select **Disable this port range** in the **Filtering mode** section. Verify that your choices look like Figure A|17 and click **OK**. Click **Add** and repeat this process with the same selections, except use ports 81 and 442, then click **OK**. Now indulge me one last time, and let's get the rest of the ports blocked by entering 444 and 65535, then click **OK** and **Finish**.

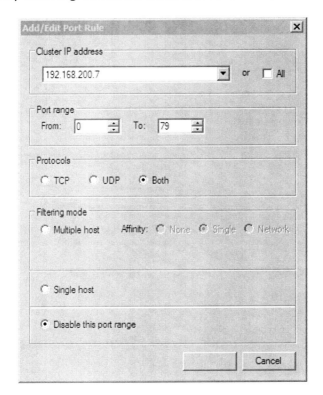

Figure A|17 > Add/Edit Port Rule

The screen shown in Figure A|18 will be displayed and the cluster will be created. You will notice your first cluster node appear beneath the cluster name in the tree view. Additional nodes can be added by right-clicking on the cluster name and selecting **Add Host To Cluster.**

Once all your IIS servers are clustered, you can control their behavior by right-clicking on the Host, selecting **Control Host** and then selecting **Start, Stop, Drainstop, Suspend,** or **Resume.** In case you're wondering, **Drainstop** continues to service active connections, but not new ones.

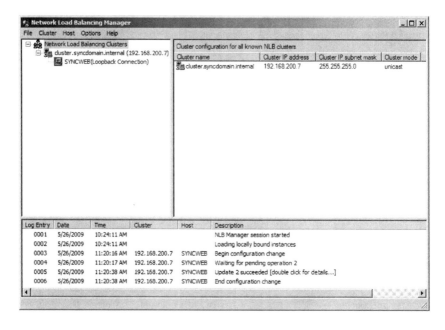

Figure A|18 > Network Load Balancing Manager

Now you know how to cluster your IIS servers; it wasn't so hard after all, was it?

Appendix B > ISA 2006 Reverse Proxy

Appendix Takeaways

As Microsoft Mobility Architects, Rob Tiffany and Michael Jimenez work with many large enterprise customers who must provide their mobile users line of business access to internal corporate application data. From an infrastructure architecture perspective, we know that enterprise data centers come in many shapes and sizes. That said, we do see data center design similarities and most of our customers have a perimeter network, or DMZ, which separates the Internet from their corporate internal corporate network. For mobility scenarios, this perimeter can help by providing internal corporate access via reverse proxy functionality so that there is management for incoming requests between the Subscribers on the Internet and IIS.

A reverse proxy server provides the following advantages over a direct connection to a Merge Replication IIS web server:

- **Security:** The reverse proxy server provides an extra protective layer between the internal network and external computers. As a security best practice, we recommend that you use a reverse proxy server so that your web server is not directly exposed to the Internet.

- **SSL encryption and acceleration:** Instead of configuring the web server to provide Secure Sockets Layer (SSL) encryption, you can offload that function to the reverse proxy server. In addition to encrypting data that is sent between the mobile device and the web server, this enables the reverse proxy server to inspect the data packets and apply filters before they reach the web server. If SSL encryption is offloaded to a proxy server, data that is sent between the reverse proxy server and the web server will not be encrypted unless SSL bridging is used.

- **SSL bridging:** If you must encrypt communication between the reverse proxy server and the IIS server, you can end the SSL session between the device and reverse proxy server, and then establish a new SSL session between the reverse proxy server and the web server. This protects the web server from direct access from the Internet, enables the reverse proxy server to filter the data packets before they reach the web server, and encrypts the data along the whole path between the device and the web server. Only the reverse proxy server will require a certificate from a reliable certification authority; the web server can use either a self-signed certificate or a certificate from an enterprise certification authority. If your reverse proxy server is connected to multiple internal servers, this may reduce certificate costs.

- **SSL offloading:** You can also terminate the SSL connection at the reverse proxy server and continue to the web server with a connection that is not encrypted. This is known as SSL offloading.

- **Load balancing:** A reverse proxy server can distribute the traffic that is destined for a single URL to a group of servers, in conjunction with Network Load Balancing.

In this section, we will focus on using Microsoft Internet Security and Acceleration (ISA) Server 2006 as a reverse proxy solution to publish SQL Server Merge Replication to mobile Subscribers. We will assume that you have ISA server already installed on a server with two network interfaces (one public-facing and one internally-facing) correctly configured in your perimeter network or Merge Replication test lab.

To learn more about ISA Server 2006, you can find a plethora of information at: http://www.microsoft.com/forefront/edgesecurity/isaserver/en/us/default.aspx.

High Level ISA Publishing Steps

- Install a server certificate on the ISA server
- Update the Public DNS
- Create the Merge Replication publishing rule using Web publishing
- Configure the ISA server with your Active Directory (LDAP) or RADIUS server set

Install a Server Certificate on the ISA Server

To enable SSL between mobile Subscribers and the ISA Server computer, you must install a server certificate on the ISA server computer. This certificate should be issued by a public Certification Authority, because it will be accessed by users on the Internet. If a private Certification Authority is used, the root Certification Authority certificate from the private CA must be installed on any device that creates a secure (HTTPS) connection to the ISA server, as well as the ISA local machine store.

The first step toward getting a Server Certificate on ISA Server is to create a certificate request from one of your IIS servers where the Server Agent is running. This is accomplished from within the Server Certificates section of the IIS Manager. In requesting the certificate, you will be required to specify various distinguished name elements including:

- Common name (FQDN)
- Organization
- Organizational unit (OU)
- City/locality
- State/province
- Country/region

You then need to select a cryptographic service provider and bit length before creating a text file that includes your certificate request. Once you get a response from a public certificate authority, and you have a certificate installed on the IIS server, you'll need to export it to a file so it can be imported into the ISA Server.

From the same Server Certificates section in the IIS Manager, you will export the certificate to a .pfx file on the IIS server. Additionally, you will provide and confirm a password to secure the .pfx file.

With the certificate exported, perform the following procedure on the ISA server computer to import the server certificate to the local computer store:

1. Copy the .pfx file you just created to the ISA server computer in a secure fashion.
2. Click **Start**, and then click **Run**. In Open, type MMC, and then click **OK**.
3. Click **File**, then click **Add/Remove Snap-in**, and in the **Add/Remove Snap-in** dialog box, click **Add** to open the **Add Standalone Snap-in** dialog box.
4. Select **Certificates**, click **Add**, and select **Computer account**; then click **Next**.
5. Select **Local Computer**, and then click **Finish**. In the **Add Standalone Snap-in** dialog box, click **Close**, and in the **Add/Remove Snap-in** dialog box, click **OK**.
6. Expand the **Certificates** node, and right-click the **Personal folder**.
7. Select **All Tasks**, and then click **Import**. This starts the **Certificate Import Wizard**.
8. On the **Welcome** page, click **Next**.
9. On the **File to Import** page, browse to the file that you previously created and copied to the ISA Server computer, and then click **Next**.
10. On the **Password page**, type the password for this file, and then click **Next**.

11. On the **Certificate Store** page, verify that **Place all certificates in the following store** is selected and that **Certificate Store** is set to **Place Cert Automatically**, and then click **Next**.   When complete, the SSL certificate should be installed in the "Personal" certificates store on the local ISA machine.
12. On the **wizard completion** page, click **Finish**.
13. Verify that the server certificate was properly installed. Click **Certificates**, and then double-click the new server certificate. On the **General** tab, there should be a note that shows you have a private key that corresponds to this certificate. On the **Certification Path** tab, you should see a hierarchical relationship between your certificate and the Certification Authority, and a note that shows **This certificate is OK.**

Update Public DNS

Create a new DNS host record in your domain's public DNS servers. Users will initiate a connection, using the name of the Web site. This name must match the common name, or Fully Qualified Domain Name (FQDN), used in the certificate installed on the ISA server computer. In this case, the following conditions must be met for the user to successfully initiate a connection:

1. The FQDN used in the server certificate installed on the ISA server computer will be merge.contoso.com.

   *It's important to note that Contoso.com is a fictitious company domain name used for demonstration purposes in this section, and is not relevant to your specific network. Remember that the certificate common name must match the FQDN.

2. The user needs to resolve merge.contoso.com to an IP address.

3. The IP address that merge.contoso.com resolves to must be configured on the external network of the ISA server computer.

Create the Merge Replication Publishing Rule

Once ISA server has been properly configured with the proper server certificates installed and DNS is updated, you can start the procedures to publish the Server Agent on the IIS server.

Launch the ISA Server Management, and within the **Firewall Policy** node, create a **New Web Site Publishing Rule** - I've called this rule, "Merge Replication Publishing Rule", as shown in Figure B|1. Click **Next**.

Figure B|1 > Web Publishing Rule Wizard

On the **Select Rule Action** screen, select **Allow,** as shown in Figure B|2, and click **Next**.

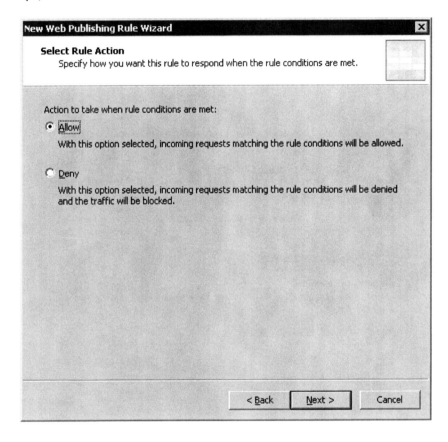

Figure B|2 > Select Rule Action

On the **Publishing Type** screen, select **Publish a single Web site or load balancer,** as shown in Figure B|3, and click **Next**.

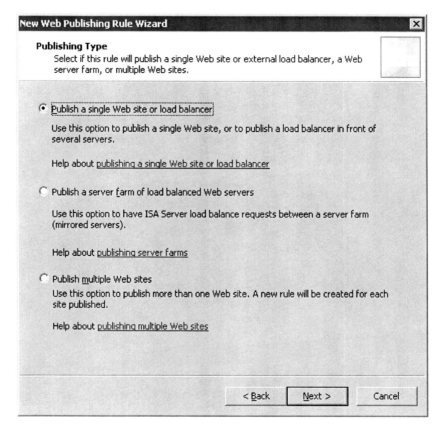

Figure B|3 > Publishing Type

On the **Server Connection Security** screen, ensure that **Use SSL to connect to the published Web server or server farm** is selected, as shown in Figure B|4. We want SSL to be used over the public network, but you don't have to use it for testing purposes. Click **Next.**

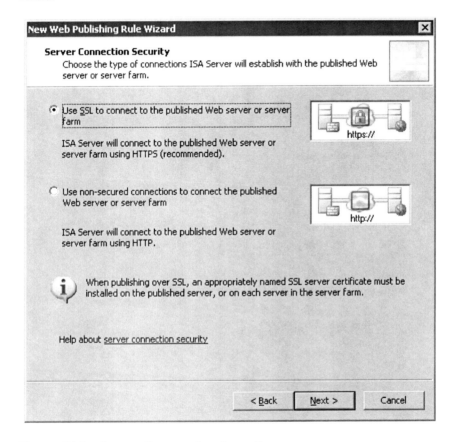

Figure B|4 > Server Connection Security

On the **Internal Publishing Details** page, specify the FQDN of the Server Agent IIS server in **the Internal site name** text box, as shown in Figure B|5. It's also a good idea to specify an IP address to connect to the IIS server. Therefore, check the check box and type the IIS server's IP address in the **Computer name or IP address** text box and then click **Next.**

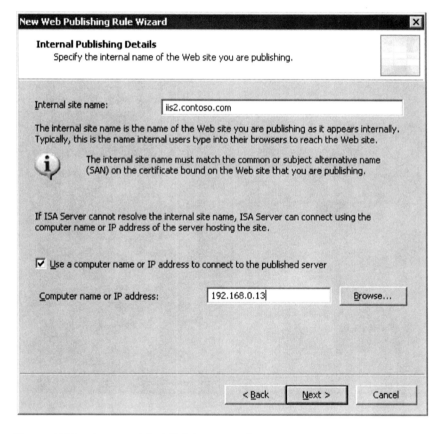

Figure B|5 > Internal Publishing Details

Further settings on the **Internal Publishing Details** screen allow you to restrict the access on this rule, by specifying the path of **/SqlCeRepl/***or **/SSCE/**, as shown in Figure B|6.

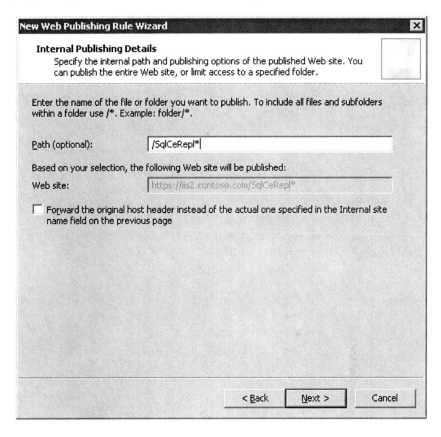

Figure B|6 > More Internal Publishing Details

On the **Public Name Details** screen, type your public DNS name, merge.contoso.com in this case, in the **Public name** text box, as shown in Figure B|7, and click Next.

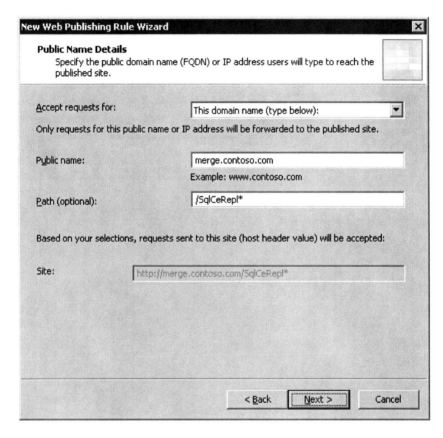

Figure B|7 > Public Name Details

On the **Select Web Listener** screen, create a listener, as shown in Figure B|8.

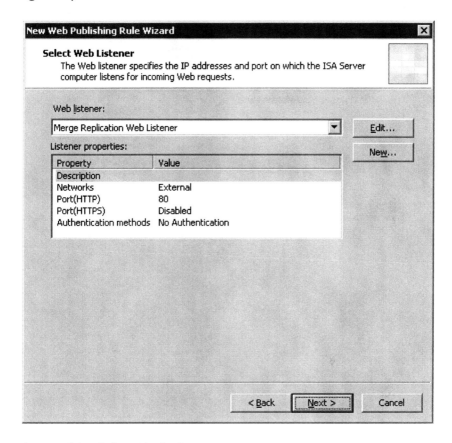

Figure B|8 > Select Web Listener

For simplicity's sake, I created an **HTTP** listener and **No Authentication**, but HTTPS & LDAP could be used. For SSL Bridging, you would need to create an SSL web listener. When validating authentication with your browser, you should be prompted for login details just once. Click **Next**.

On the **Authentication Delegation** screen, choose **No delegation, and client cannot authenticate directly**, as shown in Figure B|9 and click **Next**.

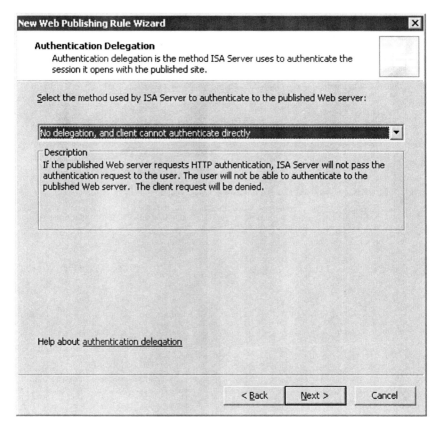

Figure B|9 > Authentication Delegation

On the **User Sets** screen, click **Add** and select **All Users**, as shown in Figure B|10.   Since we don't have authentication here, ISA can't determine users, so **All Users** is your only option.

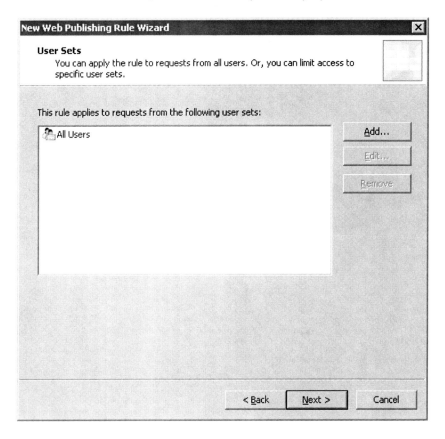

Figure B|10 > User Sets

On the **Completing the New Web Publishing Rule Wizard** screen, click **Finish** to complete the wizard, as shown in Figure B|11.

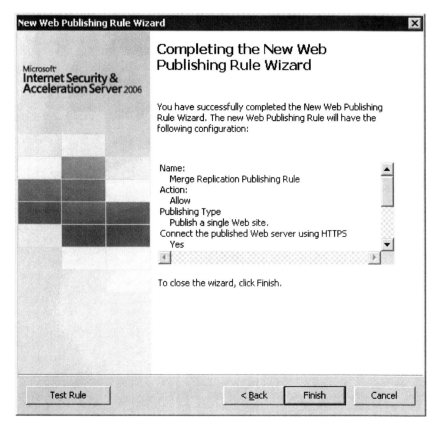

Figure B|11 > Completing the New Web Publishing Rule Wizard

After that, right-click on the rule you just created and select **Properties**. You need to change the **Link Translation** to **OFF** to resolve any potential merge replication errors. With that completed, you're all set!

Index

A

B

C

G

H

I

K

Keep in mind that this book specifically covers SQL Server 2008 running on Windows Server 2008 with SQL Server Compact 3.5 SP1 as the mobile client database., 31

L

Latency, 167
Liam Cavanagh, 12
Load balancing A reverse proxy server can distribute the traffic that is destined for a single URL to a group of servers, in conjunction with Network Load Balancing., 273

M

Maintenance, 19
MaxBcpThreads 96
Maximum Conflict 112
Maximum size of the database (in Megabytes). This can be set has high at 4091., 236, 250
Maximum size of the temporary database file (in Megabytes). This can be set has high at 4091., 236
Memory Object
  Available Mbytes 172
Microsoft, 1, 4, 8, 9, 11, 12, 13, 14, 16, 17, 27, 29, 43, 66, 148, 193, 197, 200, 215, 224, 248, 271, 273
Microsoft Sync Framework and Cloud Data Services, 12
Minimum Conflict 112
MSmerge_contents, 142, 143, 168
MSmerge_current_partition_mappings, 144, 169
MSmerge_generation_partition_mappings, 144, 169
MSmerge_genhistory, 143, 169
MSmerge_past_partition_mappings, 144, 169
MSmerge_tombstone, 142, 143, 144, 169

N

Network Load Balancing Feature, 253
New Publication Wizard, 6, 29, 99, 106, 133, 134, 141
No logging, 14, 15, 94, 167, 193, 217, 223, 227, 228, 239, 252, 266, 269

O

Ongoing Maintenance 168
Organizational unit (OU), 274
OutputVerboseLevel 96

P

Parameterized filters that filter/reduce data going to a particular Subscriber, based on a unique variable that's passed to the server by the Subscriber., 114
Performance Tuning 163, 88, 163, 222
PhysicalDisk Object
  % Disk Time
    This counter represents the percentage of time that the selected disk is busy responding to read or write requests. A value greater than 50% is an I/O bottleneck., 172
Priority Column
  Similar to the Maximum Conflict resolver, but adds support for update conflicts., 112
Processor Object
  % Processor Time
    This counter represents the percentage of processor utilization. A value over 80% is a CPU bottleneck., 172
Publication, 6, 14, 22, 23, 24, 29, 30, 97, 99, 127, 136, 137, 140, 141, 142, 143, 145, 146, 150, 151, 153, 154, 158, 160, 161, 162, 169, 170, 171, 174, 237, 240
Publication and Schema Changes, 171
Publication Properties 140, 141, 160, 171

This value specifies how many threads the Merge Agent will use to enumerate changes. Your Server-to-Server value is 3, which should work fine if your system has plenty of free processor cores to work on the task at hand., 95

T

U

Update Public DNS, 277
Upload Only
  Changes uploaded to the Publisher are accepted., 112
UploadGenerationsPerBatch 94

W

Web Properties 239

LaVergne, TN USA
25 January 2010
171112LV00004B/57/P